Son of a Yorkshire farmer, R. Neville Tate OBE's first employment was as a graduate apprentice in aeronautical engineering. However, an urge to travel led to a career change, taking up a post as a science teacher in Buenos Aires where he spent 13 years. Using the long school holidays Neville crisscrossed South America, at first by motorcycle, but later leading numerous schoolboy adventure expeditions to many of the wildest parts of that continent. Canoeing, or cycling, or horse-riding long distances demanding circumstances was often part of the package.

Returning to the UK in the mid-seventies, Neville was soon immersed in a new adventure of quite a different sort, becoming the founding headmaster of Yarm School, one of the very few "Public Schools" to be started from scratch since World War II.

Current hobbies and interests include light aircraft flying, gardening and model railways, and of course, adventure travel. Neville, as a constituency delegate addressed the 1976 Conservative Party Annual Conference and served for five years as a non-executive director of the North Tees Hospital Trust.

To all those brave parents who allowed (and even encouraged) their precious offspring to join my adventure expeditions, to their ultimate benefit. "I went a boy and returned a man" was the summary of David Hall, one of the participants.

R. Neville Tate OBE

TRANSIT TO INDIA

AUSTIN MACAULEY PUBLISHERS™

LONDON * CAMBRIDGE * NEW YORK * SHARJAH

A CIP catalogue record for this title is available from the British Library.

ISBN 9781528984683 (Paperback)
ISBN 9781528984690 (Hardback)
ISBN 9781528984713 (ePub e-book)
ISBN 9781398418332 (Audiobook)

www.austinmacauley.com

First Published 2022
Austin Macauley Publishers Ltd®
1 Canada Square
Canary Wharf
London
E14 5AA

Chapter 1

The central bazaar in Zahedan in eastern Iran, though by no means in the same league as Istanbul's Kapali Carsi or Cairo's Khan Al Khalili, was in all essentials much like its far, far bigger and more famed sisters. Yet on one particular August day in 1984, an element in Zahedan's pattern of trade made the place distinctly unique and, in its way, remarkable. For there, in cheeky openness, was a stall being run by English schoolboys. They were selling, believe it or not, tins of baked beans, of Ambrosia rice pudding and other popular standbys of the British home. These same lads were also providing cooking tips and offering free samples prepared on a tiny primus stove. Bemused locals crowded round, drawn by the novelty of the scene and brisk sales resulted.

The date held some significance. For a start August is Iran's hottest month and 1984, the Orwellian year, a sad time of war and revolution in the ancient land of Persia. An intolerant fanatic, the Ayatollah Khomeini, had returned from exile in 1979 to overthrow the authoritarian pro-Western rule of the Shah and in its place had established a revolutionary Islamic state, a regime particularly hostile to Britain and the United States. By 1984 Iran was also in the thick of a vicious war with neighbouring Iraq, then ruled by another troublesome dictator, Saddam Hussein. This titanic conflict between Shia Iran and Sunni-dominated Iraq was to claim over a million lives.

But what in the first place were these ten English schoolboys and their two teachers doing in the dusty and remote Iranian city of Zahedan in the middle of such a war?

To answer this question, I will have to take you back a few months to the small market town of Yarm in the north-east of England, where at Yarm School disappointment was being felt over the worth of an old Ford Transit minibus which the school had hoped to trade-in for a newer version of the same vehicle. But so little was the school being offered for its old faithful that I felt the deal hardly worth the bother and that we might just as well scrap it or give it buckshee to some charity. In fact, there was next to nothing wrong with it except for some ugly rusting around the wheel arches, yet such is the tyranny of modern-day attitudes that the school had little choice but to replace it for the sake of its all-important *image*. Today's parents set great store by the fripperies of equipment and facilities.

It was while mulling over these irritating issues that I remembered 'Lepra', a charity the school was regularly supporting. Leprosy is curable these days but myths and deeply rooted prejudices about the disease were still preventing many fully cured victims claiming their rightful place in society and their share of economic opportunity. This was particularly true of certain remote rural communities in India and I was aware of the vital work this charity was engaged in work as much about education as medicine. Suitable vehicles to enable Lepra's specialist personnel reach these backward communities were urgently needed yet the purchase of even one would absorb thousands of pounds from a budget where spending just a few pounds secures all the drugs necessary to save a sad victim from leprosy's cruel ruin. In short, it seemed to me ridiculous that, thanks to the crazy dictates of Western economics, we were proposing to throw away as trash exactly the sort of vehicle heroic medics in India desperately needed for their work.

Among its various clubs, societies and extra-curricular bodies, the same school ran an 'Expedition Club' which organised overseas travel and exploration for groups of pupils over the summer holidays. Most of these expeditions were built around travel in a school minibus to destinations off the beaten track and rather more exciting than those commonly accessible via the mainstream travel agencies of the time – the 1970s and 80s. Further, not only was such travel physically tough, thanks to the rather basic nature of the vehicles then available, but food and accommodation were equally of an improvised nature with primus stove cooking and camping the norm and a meal in restaurant or a night in a hotel very much the exception. I had been running such trips for a good many years and because only the basic outlines – ferry bookings and suchlike – were pre-planned, a frequent catalogue of untoward and unexpected incidents was more or less inevitable and led to an atmosphere of adventure that most boys found heady and exciting.

I don't recall the point at which a link actually formed in my mind between the minibus we had for disposal and an Indian leprosy charity's urgent need for vehicles but clearly the real eureka moment was when I realised that I could make a splendid Expedition Club adventure by physically delivering our old bus to the charity in India.

For, by filling it up with volunteer pupils and then driving all the way to India through Europe and the lands of the Middle East, I would of course be opening up for them the opportunity of once-in-a-lifetime adventure.

I will delay until later details of the bureaucratic adventures I also had to endure to obtain visas to allow us to pass through war-torn revolutionary Iran and to import into India, without customs duty, our old minibus and a small trailer. Let us for the moment just picture an elderly commonplace minibus crammed full of sweating teenagers grinding along the desert highway linking the two sweltering and dusty Iranian cities of Kerman and Zahedan. The distance between them is 317 miles (510km) and we are hoping to do it in something like nine or ten hours. The terrain is an intimidating blend of sand and bare rock as the road crosses the southern end of the formidable Dasht-e Lut desert. There are no roadside towns or settlements to divert attention or mark progress. It is a continuum of heat and glare. According to NASA's satellite research, this area holds the record for the hottest land temperatures on the planet and on occasion the ambient temperature has exceeded 70°c. At first the road was quite good but the further east we travelled the rougher it became. There was virtually no other traffic but about every half hour or so a vague form would emerge from the shimmering haze ahead and gradually assume the outline of a large truck. As it neared it would turn on its headlights and often also blast its raucous horn, these acts a precaution in case the other vehicle had a sleeping driver. We, too, for like reason adopted the custom and those pupils in the back not yet comatose would wave and cheer lustily as the vehicles passed, giving I suppose the poor devils something to do.

Twelve people on a seven-week journey require a lot of luggage and to provide as much interior space as possible for long teenage legs, most of it was either on the roof or in the trailer. Additionally, the challenging nature of the journey obliged us to carry two spare wheels for the bus as well as extra petrol, all of which is heavy stuff.

Another concomitant of self-sufficiency in desert travel is the need for a fair amount of on-board water, yet another weighty commodity. Finally, there is the question of food and the heavy gas cylinders to cook it. I'll come later to the subject of food on our journey. What is particularly relevant here is that a fair portion of it was in the form of tinned food – often in large catering size tins –

and tinned food for twelve healthy appetites takes some carrying and makes for a weighty cargo.

Our willing little trailer was a converted 'Conway' camping trailer, stripped of its original frame tent but retaining its washbasin and water tank. The sides had been built up to increase capacity and a hinged plywood top, secured with decent padlocks, rounded off its conversion to cargo box on wheels. In a perfect world our great load ought to have been carried aboard a twin axel trailer of horse-box size and sturdiness and it should have been fitted with wheels and tyres matching those of the bus.

Unhappily, our little trailer was a light single axle job with dainty nine-inch wheels and was obviously far from ideal but, bearing in mind that at our journey's end in India it would have to be given away with the bus, it was all the school budget could afford. All the way to Istanbul and well beyond our small trailer performed to perfection and it was only when badly broken and liberally potholed roads became commonplace and air temperatures soared, that troubles began to arise.

It is easy to see why. Every time a wheel falls into a pothole or bounces over a rock, the air within the tyre is compressed and rises in temperature. With a large wheel there is plenty of surface area and the extra heat is soon dissipated but with a very small one the temperature may well build up to such an extent that the fabric of the tyre is badly weakened and a puncture —or worse— quickly results.

Unfortunately, the trailer was narrower than the bus and so its woes were invisible to the driver. Moreover, the trailer's behaviour could not be easily felt through the driving controls and thus a failing tyre was seldom noticed until it had been damaged beyond repair.

The final twenty or so miles into Zahedan were a Hell of repeated stoppages forced on us by the need every two or three miles to pump up the trailer's damaged tyres, having by then used up all our several spare tyres and spare tubes. The older boys, on their own initiative, had shared out this hot and weary work, a gesture which did much for my flagging spirit. What was abundantly clear was that our little trailer was now on its last legs. Given also that the road eastward to the Pakistan frontier and the roads through Pakistan's Baluchistan province would be a good deal rougher than those we had so far experienced, it was clear that our only hope lay in a drastic reduction in the load we were asking our poor trailer to carry. It was time to take stock of our situation and we did this by the roadside over a long-delayed breakfast.

"The Pakistan frontier is still seventy or eighty miles away, Roy," I began, addressing my colleague Roy Woodforde, a beefy young teacher in his early twenties. "Our Iranian transit visas, don't forget, run out at midnight and there'll be a string of check points to get through as we near the border. So, I guess, even if we didn't have the trailer to hold us up, we could be talking of something like six hours. It's now nine thirty and it's probable the frontier will close at nightfall. Any ideas?"

"We can't abandon the trailer?"

"Even supposing we could find room in or on the bus for the essentials it's carrying, the big issue is the documents."

"How so, sir?" chipped in Craig, a tall forceful fifth former.

"The vehicle *carnet,* Craig, gives us permission to import the bus temporarily into each country we pass through, without payment of custom dues, *provided* we re-export it, whole and complete, within three months. That means *with* the trailer because to import the trailer in the first place it had to be listed on the *carnet* as part of the bus."

"And if we don't?"

"Then we are liable to three times the value of the vehicle – based incidentally on the value as new, not upon its current worth."

"You're kidding!"

"Well, what if you broke down or crashed or something and couldn't drive it out of the country?" enquired Alan, another strapping fifth former, his tone and expression suggesting we might deliberately wreck the trailer to fiddle the issue.

"Then we would have to arrange to have the wreckage exported."

"Damn," Alan exclaimed.

"And, as usual, another of your bright ideas bites the dust, Alan," grinned Craig, throwing an arm round his pal.

There was a long silence and I looked round a circle of glum, grime-streaked faces.

"All the food we are carrying, sir, must weigh a ton," announced Slackie, a boisterous fourteen-year-old whose formal handle was David Tite. "Can't we just get rid of it and then buy stuff as we go along?"

"Nobody likes it anyway," grumbled another David, Dave Armstrong. "We've all got baked beans coming out of our ears and everybody's fed up with tinned rice pudding. What's more, we all puke at just the thought of that pink death that calls itself 'luncheon meat'."

11

I had some sympathy. In my anxiety to reduce the trailer load and to save travel time by making meal stops shorter, over recent days I had been encouraging Roy to serve up tinned food. However, the tinned products we had with us did reflect the boys' stated preferences and I couldn't resist reminding them of this.

"When we said we liked baked beans, sir," countered Slackie, "we didn't mean we wanted them served up morning, noon and night, sir."

"How much should we ditch? Half?" enquired Roy, assuming the decision made. I hesitated, torn between necessity and an instinctive hatred of waste.

"I think we should get Slackie to sell the stuff in a local bazaar," suggested Phil Cairns, an athletic blond lad with a penchant for mischief. "He has the experience and, what's more, the figure for selling junk food."

An outburst of laughter and ribald comment followed, "For Goodness' sake," I began irritably, "can't you…"

"I like it," said Roy seriously. "I don't see why we can't at least give it a try. If it doesn't sell, well we just chuck it."

"You've got to be joking," I protested. But he wasn't.

The notion of selling our surplus food made an instant appeal to the boys. They saw it as go-getting and clearly sensed it would be fun. I saw it as likely to provoke both the town authorities and the traders. After all, pirate traders would be given pretty short shrift even in a quiet English market town so what chance benign acceptance in touchy and volatile Iran? However, not wanting to be a killjoy and keeping in mind I had sold our journey to India as 'lots of fun and adventure', despite my misgivings I gave way.

A few minutes later it was all settled. I would drop off Roy and six of the boys at the entrance of the main bazaar in Zahedan. Each of the six would have a rucksack or holdall crammed full of tins while Roy would carry a primus stove, spare spoons and a tin opener. Behind the stove and so on lay the notion that the locals would not be familiar with Crosse and Blackwell's beans nor with Mr Ambrosia's instant creamy rice and that to assist sales it would be a good idea to offer free samples and show how easy was the preparation of such novel delicacies. It was agreed Roy would decide what was to be disposed of and what price would be asked.

Once I had dumped Roy's party, the task for me and the remainder of the boys was to find a tyre repair place. It took well over an hour to fix the trailer tyres and when I returned to the bazaar, I found a dense crowd surrounding our merchant venturers but, to judge from the animated, laughing faces of our young salesmen, all seemed absolutely hunky-dory. I inched my way through the press until I was alongside Roy. I had never seen anything quite so incongruous as these English schoolboys running a food stall in this Persian bazaar. Two had even gone so far as to sit cross-legged on the ground, Asian fashion; one in charge of the money box and the other heating sample mouthfuls of baked beans on the primus. Meanwhile the rest were bustling about attending to customers, getting across their sales patter by means of hand signs, facial expressions and exchanges in English and Farsi. I looked about me, drinking in the details of the unforgettable spectacle and rejoicing in the boys' enjoyment of a seventh heaven. I had but one regret: I had left my camera in the bus.

Then I suddenly saw something which made my heart miss a beat as I felt the cold hand of fear.

"Roy," I called urgently. "You haven't been selling those, have you?"

He glanced quickly in the direction I pointed and grinned enthusiastically. "Yep. They've done quite well. Sold three or four I think."

"God, Roy! Don't you bloody realise? It's pork!"

"Pork? No, it's not. It says, 'Luncheon Meat'. There's nothing about pork."

"Bloody hell, man. Luncheon meat *is* pork. Everybody knows that."

"The word isn't on the tin," he muttered defensively, picking one up and looking closely at it.

"Then thank God for that! But look at the damned list of ingredients…"

He was already nodding in agreement. "Yes, pork eighty-nine percent, water…"

"Never mind how much. One percent will be enough to start a lynching."

We both studied the tight circle of our Islamic customers and bystanders. I noticed for the first time there were two policemen in the crowd. They seemed amused rather than in any way disapproving. But for how long? Roy touched my arm.

"That guy there bought one. Maybe we can buy it back."

The suggestion flashed through my mind like a sudden ray of sunshine, only to be dismissed a split second later. "No. We haven't the language. It would only draw attention to it. We've got to get out of here – and fast – before anyone cottons-on.

13

Look, I'll go and fetch the bus. Bring everything to an end but as naturally as you can. Never mind about any gear. Just make sure you have all the boys with you."

Apparently, the sudden winding up of the business had upset some would-be customers and a knot of them had surged forward, for a time surrounding some of the boys. However, Roy did a brilliant job extracting them and by the time I arrived back with the bus, there they all were, waiting. It was not a moment too soon. The two policemen had come out of their passive mode and I could tell by the way they were walking that they were minded to stop and question us.

The boys, reading the urgency of the situation, had piled into the bus like getaway bandits and as the last one tumbled aboard I let go the clutch and gently set off just as one of the policemen raised his hand and broke into a run. I looked away but resisted the urge to accelerate. Then I heard them whistle but a taxi had cut in behind us and, so shielded, I knew it was now safe to 'high tail it' out of town.

It was seventy miles to the frontier, and I guessed it would probably take us three hours or more as the road was poor. There were also several check points to pass. There was no doubt in my mind that if our 'crime' came to be discovered it would be regarded as a terrible insult and a huge diplomatic incident was just about the best outcome we could expect. The worst did not bear thinking about.

Telephone wires ran alongside the road and I even considered cutting them to stop orders to detain us reaching the check points or the border guards. The poles were quite short and I could have easily reached the wires by standing on the roof of the bus. However, criminal damage of that nature does not easily pass the conscience of a respectable headmaster and the wires remained intact. And so did we, passing safely into Pakistan and out of the jurisdiction of the Ayatollahs about 8.00 pm that evening.

Chapter 2

Scary incidents punctuated by lucky breaks, such as the one just described, would be a fair, if somewhat jaundiced, way of summing up our overland journey to India. Looking after a mobile cage of monkeys – even bright and biddable monkeys – is after all a down-to-earth affair as much about avoiding burnt sausages, diarrhoea and lost passports (not to mention lost boys!) as it is about iconic architecture, must-visit museums and breath-taking landscapes. Journeying 10,000 kilometres in a basic minibus – that is to say without air-conditioning and with bog-standard seats – is an uncommon way to spend your school holidays and it would be strange, given the nature of the countries we were passing through, if it failed to throw up a story or two. It is high time, therefore, that I began at the beginning and started setting things down in their proper order.

Given the Expedition Club's record within Yarm School of overland travel adventures, a viable number of hardy volunteers willing to travel to India with the bus soon put down their names and the business of gaining their parents' consent and support began. There were also three crucial and potentially very tricky, 'external' items to secure where failure in any degree would torpedo the whole venture. These items were: the granting by Iran of transit visas, advance permission by the Indian government to import the old bus, as a charitable donation, without payment of customs duty and appropriate insurance of the vehicle, pupils and teachers by the school's insurers. Acquiring these absolute necessities, each of which was something of a tall order, was not only time-consuming but plagued by negative attitudes that had to be fought tooth and nail.

Taking first the question of the Iranian visas, the general view at the time in all sectors of the travel industry was that without an invitation from some highly placed figure within Iranian revolutionary circles, getting visas would be next to impossible.

Quite simply the Ayatollah Khomeini did not wish to see infidel Westerners wandering about Holy Iran. However, we could only try and a telephoned request to the Iranian Consulate saw a wad of visa forms arrive at the school by return of post. Surely it wasn't going to be that easy? The forms, arrestingly headed *'In the Name of God',* were long and detailed but, duly completed and accompanied by passports and the required fees, were swiftly posted back. Four days later we received an uncompromising telephone call to say that visas would *not* be granted and that someone should call at the consulate *in person* to retrieve the passports and postal orders! No, they could not be posted back to us and it was still 'no' despite our pointing out that to traipse up to London to fetch them would involve a round trip of five hundred miles.

The Ayatollah's minions in the Iranian Consulate certainly knew how to be awkward!

The Iranian Consulate, a relatively modest terrace house in Kensington, was a scene of utter chaos. Wherever I turned there were knots of people engaged in noisy scrummages around doorways leading to the various offices and departments. Every sign and notice was in Farsi (Persian) and, as far as I could judge, every one of the pushers and shovers seemed to be an Iranian. High on the wall, opposite the front entrance, was a large portrait of the Ayatollah Khomeini – his expression of scowling disapproval entirely justified by the present behaviour of his countrymen. A man who had just damaged me with his elbow at least had the grace to apologise and in English at that.

"Would you know where the visa section is?" I asked, snatching my opportunity. "Down at the end and up the stairs."

The world upstairs was tranquil in comparison. There were still clusters of people dotted about in random confusion, but up here everyone was still, silent, and morose. In fact, nothing at all seemed to be happening until, quite suddenly, a door was thrown open and a bossy-looking woman emerged. She glanced fiercely left and right and one or two fellows in the dismal throng timidly raised a hand to attract her attention. They were wasting their time. Hissing and flinging her arm in contemptuous dismissal, she faced them down. Then she noticed me and screwed up her face as if she had just encountered a bad smell.

"Yes? What you want?"

The whole fruitless business of Iranian visas had given me nothing but grief and to cap it all, thanks to the consulate's stupid intransigence, I had been obliged to come up to London at a time when I was exceptionally busy in school. Quite

16

obviously, without Iranian visas our overland journey to India was a write-off (quite simply there was no other practicable route) and I felt bitter and disappointed. I and the other participants had fallen in love with the notion of our great overland journey to India and I was certainly in the right frame of mind to sound off about the way our application had been treated. To be honest though, taking into account all the political aspects, I entertained not the slightest hope of the decision being reversed. Now an uncanny instinct rising within me was warning me to steer clear of this dragon and urging me to stand my ground and take the matter to the highest possible level.

"The consul has given me an appointment to discuss a visa application," I blurted out. "I was told to come up here."

"The consul is not here."

"I know," I further lied. "He told me he might be away but said that if that was the case his assistant would gladly see me." I was amazed at the confident, matter of fact tone of my own voice.

"Wait," said the dragon imperiously. She frowned as if something puzzled her and then stepped back into her lair. It must have been all but an hour I was kept waiting. From time to time she would reappear but, ignoring me completely, condescendingly attend to the business of one or another of the many waiting souls. At length a spry little fellow popped out, his neat Islamic beard confined to the line of his chin and jaw. He wore a formal grey suit but, as seemed then to be the fashion among Iranians, had no tie to go with his buttoned-up shirt.

"Come," he said, gesturing to me with his hand. Once in his office I gave him no time to ask questions but instead launched into a detailed account of our proposed trip. I told him of our passion to visit Iran and said that my pupils couldn't wait to see the glorious mosques of Isfahan, the religious schools of Qom, or the carpet bazaar in Kerman. Omar Khayyam, I boasted, was their favourite poet and that the mere sight of Persian script gave them all untold delight. I went into our work for leprosy charities and spoke of our plans for when we got the bus to India. He listened through it all in cold silence, his head slightly bowed and his hands crossed on the desk. After I had finished, for quite some time he maintained the same emotionless posture before abruptly pushing the bell button on his desk. The dragon entered and the little man spoke briefly to her. Out she went, only to return moments later with a big brown envelope, dropping it on to the desk in what was an unmistakable display of annoyance and disapproval. With interminable slowness the little man shuffled through the envelope; glanced at a couple of papers and in a desultory fashion flicked through our passports. I saw that our uncashed postal orders were still attached. Suddenly he looked up.

"I am sorry. Something is wrong. We have many preoccupations at the moment and your visas have not been prepared." He spoke with infinite weariness. "You must come back in the morning. I will have them ready for you."

Don't ask me how or why it happened. All I know is that things sometimes go like that with the bureaucracies of authoritarian regimes. I had had several similar experiences over the years when I had lived in Latin America. In such situations I don't bother my head with the ins and outs of it but just sigh with relief and move on.

The miracle of the Iranian visas created in me an illogical but powerful feeling that we were somehow *meant* to get to India. Without this I don't think I could have coped with India's stonewalling obfuscation. To get acceptance that a vehicle donated *for free* to an Indian charity should not pay Indian customs duty generated a file of correspondence over two inches thick. It embraced letters of commendation from the leprosy charities involved, both in the UK and in India. Umpteen departments of the Indian government and of their UK High Commission, a firm of public notaries and the school's bankers all, willingly or unwillingly, had to make their contribution. Even a letter from the Ford Motor Company was demanded to confirm that conversion of a Transit minibus to an ambulance was technically feasible. Only Uncle Tom Cobley seemed to escape the great game pursued by Delhi's tireless bureaucrats.

Overland travel back in 1984 to Turkey and beyond also involved extracting transit visas from the suspicious and graceless consulates of the Soviet regimes of Eastern Europe. Hungary and Yugoslavia were fine, Rumania and Bulgaria something else. Departure was only a week away when the last documents in our six-month paper chase finally came to hand.

Such a lengthy journey, especially when extensive swathes of it would involve rough roads over mountains and scorching deserts, obviously exposes the vehicle to punishing abuse. Our minibus was already ten years old and, even before it had been acquired by the school, had endured years of hard usage as a hire vehicle. Bearing in mind that the poor old thing would be heavily laden as well as required to tow a trailer, the question of what we might do to minimise the chance of a catastrophic breakdown, doubtless in some desolate spot in the

18

middle of nowhere, loomed large in my thoughts. My answer was to organise a vehicle maintenance course as one of the school's summers terms 'activity options', using the India minibus as the course 'guinea pig' and a local garage mechanic as the course teacher. It proved a popular 'activity option' and three members of the India party were among the attendees. In this way we not only got the mechanical aspects of the bus thoroughly checked over and serviced, but we also put ourselves in the fortunate position of having three freshly instructed young maintenance 'experts' travelling in the party.

But it wasn't only our bus which had to be kept fit. The boys would be travelling, heaped together in a hot, dusty and cramped vehicle for six or more weeks. Sleeping, for the most part, would be in the open under the stars. They would have to contend with flies and mosquitoes. Their food would be a mix of local purchases and rations carried from the UK. Water supplies at times were sure to be difficult and in all their eating and drinking the youngsters would have to face the delights of Asiatic hygiene. And all this before spending two weeks or so in the Indian sub-continent itself, a part of the world notorious for gruesome afflictions of stomach and bowel. School trips, of course, have to take place in school holidays and only the summer break is long enough to accommodate so many weeks of solid travelling. August in the Persian deserts and highlands means routine temperatures of 40°C and highs of over 50! And just as discouraging, by the time we reached India the monsoon would be in full spate and hardly providing good camping weather! The youngest boy in our party was twelve; most were about fourteen and the oldest were sixteen. Children in all conscience. Matters of health, I kept reminding myself, would have to receive great and continuous attention. In all this, of course, we received much advice and practical assistance from both the school doctor and our local hospital.

Exactly a week before the great day of departure, everyone had had his last injection and everyone had started taking his daily dose of anti-malaria tablets. The final itinerary had been circulated and arrangements for emergency contact had been worked out (of course no mobile phones in 1984) and talked over with the parents. Roy Woodforde, my co-leader and the expedition's second teacher, had all the food and medical supplies in hand and all the equipment set aside ready for loading. In all essentials we were ready for our departure on July 17th.

The blow fell during the BBC 9 o'clock News of Friday July 13th. Having dealt with a couple of international news stories, the newscaster turned to affairs in Britain where the main item was news of a looming dock strike. In my mind's

19

eye I was complacently picturing cargo ships at some great port with the dockside cranes idle and rowdy pickets at the gates. It felt good to think that we would soon be leaving such negative nonsense behind us. Then I heard the word 'Dover' and a cold hand seemed to grip my heart as the news item unfolded. Early the following week, on the very day we were booked to cross to France, a major dock strike affecting *all the Channel ports* was scheduled to begin. As both sides in the dispute had broken off talks it was impossible to say how long the strike might last but the BBC's Industrial Relations correspondent thought it would be a matter of weeks rather than days. The same man went on to explain that whilst pickets had undertaken not to hinder foot passengers using the ferries, they would be out in force to prevent the loading of vehicles.

Given the tight itinerary we had for our journey to India, the loss of even a week would be very serious. Of course, in 1984 there was no Channel Tunnel and therefore no alternative to the ferry, so our only hope lay in bringing forward our date of departure to beat the strike. If only life were that simple! Unsurprisingly, lots of other people had the same idea and a free-for-all to secure a place on the pre-strike ferries developed virtually overnight, forcing the ferry operators to organise a system of priorities. Lorries carrying food were given first priority and scheduled tour buses were placed second. Private cars and non-food freight were to be low priority. Might our minibus, I wondered with laughable optimism, somehow also count as a tour bus?

All our lovely plans for loading the minibus and trailer 'scientifically' also fell victim to the chaotic scramble to get away and we found ourselves joining Dover's manic queues only eight hours short of the strike deadline. The first harbour official we came across wanted to place our minibus-plus-trailer combination in the same category as a car and caravan, which was just about the lowest priority of all. Waving our public transport passenger manifest (a document required for our transit through Iron Curtain countries) I protested, arguing that our vehicle was documented as a bus and should be so treated. The fellow shook his head vigorously and called over a more senior colleague. I repeated my argument and once again there was a vigorous and negative shaking of an official head.

"No sir, buses carry forty or so passengers. I don't know what you are but you're not a bus. Look, wait over there by those two Land Rovers until I…"

He broke off in response to a hail from yet another loading official and then darted off.

Over to my left a line of coaches was moving slowly forward. Sheerings, Wallace Arnold, Scott Brothers, National Express. The big names. The professionals. A parade of the great and the good. But their procession lacked perfect precision and a gap opened up between Wallace Arnold and the Scott Brothers. Dare I? I gunned the engine and we shot across the tarmac. My footwork and steering were nimble and we just squeezed into the line. In no time at all we were on a long narrow ramp and descending into the cavernous jaws of the ferry. Then suddenly there was a problem. It seemed we lacked the magic letter 'J' on our windscreen. I shoved our tickets under the loading marshal's nose. "Well," he must have thought, "at least they've paid." The bus behind was revving impatiently and, anyway, jamming up the ramp as we were, what was the poor man to do with us? So, he waved us forward and we ended up somewhere in the bowels of the ship, frighteningly hemmed in on all sides by giant coaches. But, triumphantly aboard the ferry!

Chapter 3

We found a decent campsite just outside Calais and spent a good part of the subsequent day unloading and then properly reloading both the minibus and the trailer. Pleasant stops were made at Sedan and at Ulm, in Germany, where we climbed the 768 steps that took us to the top of the cathedral's 530-feet high spire, the tallest in Europe. This is reached by a dizzying open staircase but the view, in glorious July sunshine, made the effort worthwhile and stretched over the Danuban landscape as far as Bavaria and the snow-capped Alps. Thrilling as the spire is, this great church is also famed for its wood carvings and other medieval treasures.

After a night spent camping on the banks of the Danube, our next call was Munich. There is much to see in such an historic and wealthy city and we were set to spend about six hours there. The big question was where to park. The minibus with its trailer was almost thirty feet long, so it was hardly the ideal vehicle for cruising round in the heavy traffic of a city centre, particularly given the low impatience threshold of many German drivers.

Landshuter Strasse was a two-lane one-way street. Aware I was likely to travel a touch slower than the Mercedes-Benzes and BMWs swarming around me, I opted for the right-hand lane, little realising that this was dedicated to vehicles heading for an underground car park. By the time the penny dropped our lane had slowed to a walking pace whereas in the one to our left the traffic was zooming past, making it difficult to change over.

"Headmaster," called Roy from the back. "Why don't you stay in this queue? We might as well park here. You'll never find ordinary street parking for a thing our length in a month of Sundays."

"Good thinking, Mr Woodforde."

In point of fact I don't like underground or multi-storey car parks at the best of times and their tight turns and cramped bays are no place for a large car let alone a minibus and trailer. Still, in the circumstances I had to acknowledge it was our best option.

Ahead there was a flashing neon sign and by common consent among our GCSE- German-learning youth, the sign was telling us spaces were available. There was also a notice which needed no German to understand: the headroom was 2m 90.

"Quickly, someone," I called over my shoulder. "How high in Christian numbers is two meters ninety?"

There was a silent delay and then a sudden flood of discussion. Somebody demanded the loan of a pencil.

"Hurry up for goodness' sake." There was now only one car between us and the entrance. More busy whispering.

"It'll be OK," said Roy confidently.

"Grab the ticket, James." The machine was, of course, sited for left-hand drive.

The interior was vast and yet, having circled right round, it was clear there wasn't even a hint of a space. "We'll have to try the lower deck."

The ramp was narrow and steep, but it was well lit and I drove down in some confidence, leading the long line of cars which we had gathered in our wake. There was a sharp turn at the bottom and the instant I had rounded the corner I knew it was journey's end. The last bit of the ramp was spanned by a great concrete beam, and it was obvious at a glance that in no way could we pass under it.

Reversing with a trailer is never easy. Reversing with a trailer which cannot be seen because it is narrower that the towing vehicle is a good deal harder. Reversing round a corner with a trailer heaps on the difficulty in logarithmic progression and doing so uphill adds still further to the challenge. The real fun begins, however, when you try to get a long line of impatient Germans to play their part by putting their own vehicles into reverse.

It wasn't many seconds before we were in real trouble. The problem was the ramp was too narrow to permit me to swing the minibus out enough to get the trailer to go in the right direction and so in no time at all it had jack-knifed.

"Listen chaps," I shouted above the cacophony of blaring car horns, "you'll have to get out. uncouple the trailer and push it back up the ramp."

There was a fair amount of banter and mock protest but everyone quickly buckled down to doing what was required.

"Alan Beattie and Dave Armstrong speak the best German, Roy. Tell them to explain things to the drivers so as to get them to reverse and let us out."

This operation went very badly. As is often the case with schoolboys, they were extremely reluctant to expose their imperfect German to native ears. As Roy put it to me later: "You'd have thought from their pathetic reaction that I was asking them to sing 'Colonel Bogey' to the Gestapo." At length I went back myself and in loud English, supplemented by appropriate gesticulation, made it clear to the near-apoplectic Teutonics that whatever the rights and wrongs of the situation, their only hope of reaching home before nightfall was to behave like sensible chaps and organise a systematic reversing of all the cars in the queue. It was at this point I received further bad news.

"Er…Neville," said Roy mopping his sweat-streaked face. "The ramp is too steep for us. The boys and I can't push the brute of a trailer against the slope. We could do with the help of a couple of beefy Germans."

"Well, you ask them, Roy. They've heard all they want to hear from me." Roy somehow succeeded in recruiting three well-built, impeccably dressed

German businessmen. Red-faced from anger and frustration at the start of their exertions, they were ashen and glaze-eyed at the finish and it was a miracle we did not witness at least one cardiac arrest.

Even the most tangled of cords, given time, end up straight and knot-free and so at length we emerged from that ill-starred edifice towing the trailer and with all our passengers aboard. A policeman had appeared and he authoritatively held up the traffic in the street to let us out. Just as I was about to accelerate away, a man stepped in front of us and signalled for me to stop. I recognised him as one of the car drivers we had just been upsetting.

"Excuse me, sir," he said courteously in excellent English, a puzzled frown on his face and his head shaking negatively from side to side. "Could you kindly explain something to me?"

"Certainly, I will if I can."

"I have just spent almost half an hour witnessing a very illuminating incident."

"And?" I prompted, wondering what on earth he was leading up to.

"And you are all English, yes?"

"Er…yes we are."

The head shaking became more marked. "Then, sir, I just do not understand how ve managed to lose the var."

The stunningly beautiful road from Munich to Salzburg put us in the right frame of mind for enjoying the baroque glories of this most lovely Austrian city, the birthplace of Mozart and still today a place brim-full of musical events and festivities. Salzburg also happens to have a small campsite right in the city centre: a great boon and saving the tiresome daily traipse in from distant suburbs which is the camper's lot in most cities. Needless to say, I used the visit to inflict serious doses of culture on the boys, giving them prepared handouts on Salzburg's history and architecture before we set out. First, I herded them round the Benedictine abbey of St Peter, a Romanesque Basilica dating from 1143 which was remodelled in the richest rococo style in the eighteenth century. Its onion-domed tower and elegant cupola, which were added at the same time, are still today key elements in Salzburg's beguiling skyline. Tours of the Franciscan church, of Mozart's birthplace, of the archbishop's palace, including the Residenz itself with its great art gallery; and finally, the Getreidegasse, Salzburg's charming 'picture-book' street, were all crammed into the first day. But even the best of schoolboys easily fall victim to cultural indigestion, so as a prophylactic countermeasure we rounded things off at the Glockenspiel Cafe scoffing masses of Austrian chocolate cake to the enchanting tones of Archbishop Johann Thun's historic carillon ringing out across the square.

The next morning was spent going over the Hohensalzburg Fortress, said to be Europe's largest fully preserved medieval castle. It stands atop a small mountain and dominates the whole city and, saving ourselves hundreds of feet of laborious climbing, we zoomed to its never-breached-in-war ramparts by means of its funicular railway.

Although the boys claimed that the castle's torture chamber was disappointing, asserting with hard-bitten candour that the Museum of Torture in York was far better, all in all the castle visit gained their approval.

Not so my proposal to tour the cathedral after lunch. Indeed, there was a suppressed but unmistakable groan of dissent when I suggested they buy themselves a snack lunch somewhere and then met Mr Woodforde and me in the cathedral square at three o'clock.

"Does that mean we'll have free time to go where we like after three?" asked Slackie in feigned misunderstanding.

"No, at 3 o'clock David we're going to look round the cathedral for an hour or so and then, if all is well (teacher speak for 'provided you co-operate and behave yourselves') you will then be free to look round the city on your own.

The word 'cathedral' drew pained expressions and a mumble or two, but I affected not to notice."

"By the way *I've* arranged for a special guide – an expert on Mozart's music – to show us round. And one more thing: long trousers and clean-looking shirts for the cathedral, so allow for time to go to the campsite to change." There were further scowls to which I responded with an indulgent smile!

Our guide, Wayne Mason, was a young American musicologist who had been studying and teaching in Salzburg for some years. Heavily built, with a scholar's slight stoop, his rimless glasses, round expressive face, mop of frizzy hair and puce velvet jacket all combined to present the perfect image of what he was – a university professor. He began with a loud voice explanation of the Italian frescos which decorate the main supporting arches of this sumptuous church. After a full tour of the building, he led us back to the intersection beneath the dome where each of the four massive supporting columns carries an elevated organ console. There, quite without warning or ado, Mason threw open a tiny door let into the base of one of the columns, ducked in and disappeared! Moments later, to our complete astonishment he reappeared, standing now in front of an organ keyboard on a balcony some fifteen feet or so above us. Leaning over like a preacher, he described Salzburg's unique organ landscape before going on to stress these were the very instruments on which most of

Mozart's church music had been composed. But the best was yet to come. Courteously thanking his audience – now augmented by dozens of other visitors who had tacked on to our party – for their attention, Wayne then sat himself down at the keyboard and launched into an impromptu recital. It was a spellbinding experience: not only the incomparable setting and of course the noble music so expertly played but also his constant involvement of the boys by his astute questions and supportive feedback. Our privileged tour ended with the boys being invited up, a few at a time, to sit where Mozart himself had sat, creating his immortal works.

As we were saying our goodbyes to our professor, a frail, hunchbacked old lady hobbled up and spoke to him in German. He then turned to me:

"The lady is asking if your boys are at a seminary studying for the priesthood." For an instant I was so thrown I must have worn a look of jaw dropped vapidity.

Not so Slackie. Taking the old lady's little hand in his own two large ones and looking into her eyes, he said swiftly and gently (in German): "Yes, it is our destiny."

Minutes later when, bemused rather than disapproving, I taxed Slackie about the incident, he simply replied: "She reminded me of my Gran, sir, so I made her happy…'cos…well, I told her what she wanted to hear."

Chapter 4

We reached Vienna and made the Schonbrunn Palace the main focus of our visit. Built to rival Versailles – which it failed to do this 1441 room palace is nonetheless hugely atmospheric and exudes the ghostly dust of the long-gone Austro-Hungarian Empire. The Empress Maria Theresa had held her court here and Napoleon had arrogantly lodged himself in it in 1805 to emphasise his post-Austerlitz humiliation of the House of Hapsburg. In the corridors where we now walked, Prince Metternich had once stridden as he manipulated the kings, tsars and emperors of Europe. But for me the most clingy ghost in this palace of ghosts was that of the Emperor Franz Joseph. He had lived in the Schonbrunn for 86 years, 68 of them as the enormously conscientious; but sad, lonely and burdened, ruler of an increasingly troubled empire. Dying in 1916, at least he was spared the final humiliation of Austria's disastrous defeat and the end of both its monarchy and its empire in 1918.

The second capital of the Dual Monarchy, as the Austro-Hungarian Empire was often titled, was Budapest, which we reached a day after leaving Vienna. At the time of our journey Budapest was, of course, within the *People's Republic of Hungary*. Back in the days of Soviet Russia there was always something nerve tingling about entering an Iron Curtain country. At that time the notion of two mutually hostile superpowers was real enough and, as we were repeatedly reminded at the time, both sides had their hands perpetually hovering over their respective nuclear buttons. The Soviet satellites were especially paranoiac about spies and reactionary agents and had very arbitrary ways of handling visitors whose behaviour annoyed or worried them. Behind the Iron Curtain people who upset the authorities really did disappear, forced labour camps really did exist and let's not kid ourselves otherwise, life for most people in the Soviet bloc was grim economically and extremely bleak in terms of personal liberty. For safety's sake I felt I ought to put our youngsters in the picture over these things and inevitably this led me to make some generalised observations about the Eastern bloc which were not matched by what we experienced in Hungary, by far the most liberal of the Soviet satellites.

28

Indeed Budapest, in contrast with the respectable worthiness of Salzburg and Vienna, projected a sense of gaiety which strongly appealed to my youthful charges. The castle district of Buda, a fascinating labyrinth of cobbled streets and pavement cafes throbbed with laughing students and good-time visitors who then, in 1984, were mainly Eastern bloc people enjoying Hungary's rather relaxed form of communism. In that period, of course, no government of a Soviet satellite would have dreamt of allowing its citizens to visit Western Europe. Obviously in such company our party very much stood out and wherever we went friendly folk eagerly questioned us about life in Britain. Generally, the level of English among the youngsters we met was staggeringly good (the Communist regimes took education very seriously) and language difficulties rarely got in the way of either earnest discussion or friendly banter.

There is much to see in the highly captivating old part of Buda and more or less on arrival we had taken a cruise along the Danube (which really was blue at the time of our visit), rambled all over the Fisherman's Bastion (Halaszbastya) – a twentieth century Disneyesque pile of turrets, castellations, arches and terraces which could easily be taken as a restored medieval fortress – and dutifully toured the historic Matthias Church, which gracefully towers over the Old City. But we had not yet visited the Paris-like boulevards of Pest on the opposite side of the Danube.

"Sir," said Dave Armstrong, a cheerful and reliable boy, who at fifteen was already just about as strong and stocky as his farmer father. It was our second day in Budapest and were enjoying midmorning refreshments at a cafe overlooking the elegant equestrian statue of Saint Stephen, the 11th century Magyar hero who had turned

Hungary into a Christian country. "Well David?"

"Bradley, Beattie and me have been talking to those guys over there, sir and they've offered to show us round Pest. They say we'd go by tram and it would take about two or three hours."

The four he indicated looked to be about eighteen and were enjoying beers and cigarettes at a nearby table. Adam Beattie and Craig Bradley were sitting with them, chattering happily. I couldn't help but admire the soundness of their strategy in selecting David as their delegate. He enjoyed a reputation for being level-headed and sensible whereas the other two, though decent lads at heart, were known to be a bit of a handful.

"Sounds a good plan, David. Maybe we could all go."

His brow clouded just a touch on hearing my second sentence. "I think they meant just the three of us, sir. We're getting along using German. Two of them didn't do English at school."

"Are they at university now?"

"Yes, I think so, sir."

"Well let me have a word with Mr Woodforde and see what he wants to do over the next couple of hours."

Here was the classic dilemma of the overseas school excursion. The boys, especially the older ones, one could understand readily enough would be keen to shake off adult supervision and 'do their own thing'. Probably not exactly intending a premeditated 'painting of the town red', but with rather older Hungarian students setting the pace, how could I doubt my fifteen-and-sixteen-year-olds would be hugely keen to keep up with them? The formula hardly appealed to the schoolmaster in me. On the other hand, I reminded myself, opportunities for mixing with local people are what overseas visits should be all about.

"Hang it all, Roy," I concluded moments later, "I sell my crazy tours as *full of adventure*'. Where's the adventure if I'm with them every damned minute?"

"Too true. But do you still want me to go with the older ones and with these Hungarian lads?"

"Yes, if you don't mind. One stage of freedom at a time, if you see what I mean. Meanwhile, I'll take the five younger ones round the parliament building and then we'll all meet up here at, say, four, ready to hit the road."

I was well aware I'd left Roy with a tricky task but as a young teacher in his early twenties I felt he would be more in tune with the student outlook of our new Hungarian friends than would I. At all events, they returned on time, though flushed and excited and smelling strongly of beer. Roy had his arm round the shoulders of one of the Hungarians; both of them smoking cigars for all that Roy was not normally a smoker at all. Several additional young Hungarians, many of them very good-looking girls, had also been acquired. There were numerous rounds of hugs and handshakes before I could get our party settled into the bus and just as I started the engine a laughing young thing dropped a bottle of Tokay into my lap. All the way down from the castle hill until we reached the Elisabeth Bridge, our new friends ran alongside the bus, noisily slapping the body panels, blowing kisses and shouting cheery farewells.

"Your little gang seems to have made quite an impression on the locals, Mr Woodforde," I observed as we accelerated into the main traffic flow.

"Sir," shouted Craig from the back of the bus. "May I tell you something?"

"Go ahead Craig."

"It wasn't us that made the impression, sir. It was Mr Woodforde. If we hadn't been with him, sir, anything might have happened."

"He's right, sir," chorused other voices. "You should have seen the way he chatted up the girls, sir."

"Well Mr Woodforde," I chaffed. "Are you able to refute these charges?"

"All I can say is that it is strange how the atmosphere here in Hungary seems to affect the memory."

"How do you mean, sir?" demanded Craig.

"Well, I've just remembered it's your turn tonight, Craig, for washing up duty!"

"How very Eastern bloc!" murmured Adrian Meynell, another sixteen-year-old.

"Hard labour for speaking the truth."

Chapter 5

Rumania was very different and we knew it the instant we arrived at the frontier. Until we had reached Hungary we had not so much as waved our passports at any border crossing and even then passport stamping, visa checking and vehicle documentation had only taken the Hungarian authorities a few minutes; everything being conducted with cheerful courtesy. But here, not ten yards into Rumania, the whole atmosphere had changed. A line of shabby, wretched-looking people, many of them burdened by trussed-up overfilled suitcases or shapeless cloth bundles, caught my eye. Who were they and why were they shuffling so dejectedly into that ramshackle building? And the whole place thick with police, all to a man swarthy and scruffy and just hanging around doing damn-all. Why so many? A couple of buses and five or six cars were lined up ahead of us. I drew up behind them, switched off the engine and got out, intending to find out what we were supposed to do.

I found that the other cars were all from Poland or Hungary and were heading for various Black Sea resorts, the equivalent of the Costa Bravo for the travel-restricted citizens of Warsaw Pact countries. The cars were all Trabants; a product of communist East Germany's moribund car industry and pretty well ubiquitous throughout the Eastern Bloc during the seventies and eighties. Powered by a 600cc air-cooled two-stroke, an engine better suited to a lawnmower than a car, the Trabant was a vehicle of monumental crudity and, hard to credit but true, had a body made of papier mâché. On Balkan highways, broken down Trabants, bonnets raised and clouds of black smoke rising from the engine-bay were almost as common as signposts. Yet for all its shortcomings the 'Trabby' was the only car an ordinary family in the Soviet satellites could hope to acquire and even then, a ten year wait to get one was about normal.

A shrill whistle arrested my attention and I saw that the police wanted me to move our minibus alongside the customs house. I quickly obliged.

"All out, go zair," shouted a large policeman of operatic appearance: dark glasses, big droopy moustache, sinister expression and a uniform bearing an improbable amount of gold braid. He pointed peremptorily at a door labelled 'Immigration Police'.

We emerged ten or fifteen minutes later to find police crawling all over the bus and half its contents strewn about on the ground.

"Is there anything in particular you would like to look at?" I asked the operatic policeman. I was employing clenched teeth courtesy in a desperate effort to curb my soaring temper.

"Everysing. Everysing out. *Ve* look ven your bus is correct."

"Everything?" Screeched several boys in incredulous unison.

"Everysing. And from zer roof and from zer…" He shrugged and pointed to the trailer with his cane.

"They're mad," spat Adrian in a voice of loud dismissive contempt. Adrian; tall, dark and of outstanding intelligence, at sixteen was at the stage when a bright youngster begins to see adults and their world for what they really are, warts and all. In the seesaw world of burgeoning manhood, Adrian could be as arrogant and infuriatingly opinionated as he could be pleasant and respectful. He turned to his friends and several supported his contention with uncomplimentary comments of their own.

"Ssh, shhhh, shush. It's no use getting their backs up. Just do as they ask," I urged, anxious to nip the rebellion in the bud. "Adrian and you Dave, climb onto the roof and hand down the bags to the police."

"But sir, we spent hours this morning sorting out all…" He caught my eye and blew out his breath noisily. "OK. Bags down it has to be."

It was now my turn to be provoked. "Keys!"

The same charming pear-shaped policeman was now standing by the trailer and tapping it impatiently with his cane. I walked towards him intent on removing the padlocks but as I reached the trailer, he stopped me by pushing his cane into my chest.

"Just zer keys. You no. You vait zair." He snatched them from me and waved me away. I was now almost incandescent but managed to rein myself in. The last thing I wanted was for us to be refused entry. A few moments later Roy came up to me.

"You're wanted. There's trouble!"

He led me into an office where a bunch of our boys were looking on as two policemen and a white-coated customs woman were examining one bag after another. Their modus operandi was simple: pick up the bag, turn it upside down and spill the contents onto the tabletop, rummage roughly among the said contents and remove such items as aroused interest or suspicion.

"Sir," shouted James Gill, as he caught sight of me, his voice high pitched with indignation. "Do you see what they're doing to our luggage?"

"Yes and they've gone off with all Alan's books," chipped in someone else before I could comment.

"Where is Alan now?" asked Roy, looking puzzled.

"That cop with the big tash took him over to where they did our passports."

I turned to my colleague. "You keep an eye on things here. I'll go over and see what's bugging them." I lowered my voice. "Whatever happens, Roy, don't let the boys wind these guys up."

I found Alan and his friend Craig standing glumly by the passport counter whilst at the other side of the divide a huddle of police was busy conversing. One was using the telephone and from the way he kept glancing at the two boys it was clear they were the subject of the call.

"What's happened, chaps?"

"Sir," answered Alan, "they were going through my bag and found some books which they say I shouldn't have." He sounded bitter and resentful.

"What books?"

"Well…er…just books," he replied vaguely. A sudden suspicion flashed into my mind.

"Not something pornographic I hope?"

"Pornographic? Oh no sir. Just books like the ones you told us to bring."

Using that wonderful flair schoolboys have for the instantaneous projection of unspotted innocence, his expression said: "Pornographic? Well, I have *heard* of the term but as for me possessing or even wanting to possess such material, well, I hardly know what to say. *Surely* you can't be serious?"

The boys had been told to pack a paperback novel to while away any dull moments.

"Is something the matter?" I called across the counter. "What do you want these boys for?" The pear-shaped chief sauntered over, watchful and hostile, like a ringmaster approaching a disobedient animal.

"He," he said, pointing at Alan, "have with him prohibited zings. *Very* serious. Why you permit him?"

"What things?"

Without even deigning to turn round, the chief raised an arm and made a slight finger movement over his shoulder and one of his men came up and placed four books on the counter.

"Anti-socialist propaganda!" He stabbed the picture on the cover of the top book with an aggressive forefinger and then turned round and re-joined his colleagues, his entire body language saying: "What more evidence do you need than that?"

The book was entitled 'Stalingrad' and its cover sported a lurid picture of a World War II battle scene. Unfortunately, the picture's central feature showed a grim-visaged SS soldier bloodily bayoneting a fresh-faced Red Army hero. Ironically, as was immediately clear from reading the blurb, the book was in fact a very racy account of Soviet heroism and ultimate triumph.

"Well?" asked Roy as the three of us re-joined the group about twenty minutes later. Everyone was lolling about and clearly bored stiff. The bus had not been reloaded.

"No joy on reloading the bus?"

"Nope. They say we must wait for the chief to OK it. And you?"

"Even worse. You won't believe it but they're saying that that book Alan is reading – that one of his about Stalingrad – is anti-Soviet propaganda. I've explained and argued but they won't have it."

"So, what's next?"

"Well, I told them to confiscate the dratted thing if it worried them so much but no, of course that would be too simple. They are saying an offence might have been committed, so, to give their bored little minds something to do they are going to look further into this mountainous molehill. So, they've now sent for a translator to come from Oradea and when he gets here, he will read the book and give a ruling."

"Christ! How long is all that going to take?"

"There's no telling. Several hours." I ran my eye over the youngsters. Bored, fed-up and not really understanding what was going on. "However," I added, injecting a dose of realism into the equation, "I'm afraid our chaps' will have to get used to this sort of thing because this certainly won't be the last awkward frontier we'll have to cross."

"Right Roy," I concluded after a few seconds' thought. "We'll cook a meal and we'll repack the bus."

"What, you mean set up the stove and all that? The Rumanians are not going to like that."

"They can't expect us to spend hours and hours here without eating."

Roy shrugged his doubts. "And reloading? They've already said we're not to."

I put my head close to his and lowered my voice. "The boys are cheesed off with all this hanging around. Better to get them doing something even if, in the end, the police make us take it all out again."

The translator arrived by bus about three hours later and turned out to be a pleasant, attractive young female. After spending only a few minutes in the police building, she emerged into the sunshine carrying the suspect volumes under her arm.

"I'm sorry about this," she apologised, coming up to me. "It's just ridiculous but this is how my country is. They want me to read all the books and make a report. I shall be as quick as I can, but I must make some show of reading. I think two hours will be enough and then when I say the books are no problem, I think they will accept it."

I warmly expressed my thanks. "We still have the currency to sort out and we will need a little time for that, so perhaps your two hours won't seem too long."

"Currency? Oh…that may also cause you problems," she said with concern in her voice. "Would you like me to come with you and talk to them?"

"Gosh…would you? That will be wonderful."

It was as well that Elena, as our friendly translator was called, came with me.

Rumanian currency regulations in the bad old Ceausescu days required all foreign visitors to convert a minimum of 10 US dollars into Rumanian *lei* at the official rate for each day spent in the country. We already knew about this but had been told by the Rumanian consulate in London that this only applied to those over the age of eighteen and, therefore, only Roy and I should have been involved. However, the officials here at the frontier were insisting this was not so and demanded 10 dollars a day from each and every one of us. The sum may not appear much at first sight, but the country was so rundown and poverty stricken that it would be difficult for us to find anything each day to spend 140 dollars on!

"Have you got any cigarettes?" Elena asked me in an abrupt aside while she was conversing with a couple of surly-looking officials.

"For you…or do you mean for them?"

"Them. It will help."

"I have a pack of L & Ms"

"No Kent?"

"No."

"The L & M will do."

When I returned with the pack Elena was smiling. "Ten dollars for you and the other teacher and for four of the boys. It is not correct but it is the best I can do."

By the time we had cleared the last of Rumania's spurious formalities we had spent almost seven hours at the frontier and had, in effect, lost a whole day's travel. We offered Elena a lift back to Oradea, which was on our route, but she declined, wryly admitting that while she would have to wait until late in the evening to get home on the one and only bus, travelling in a foreign vehicle would land her in serious trouble.

State-imposed restrictions and frustrations in the Soviet bloc satellites were by no means confined to entry formalities at the border. Foreign registered vehicles were subject to route restrictions, stops at certain check points and various other bothersome rules unknown to travellers in Western Europe. In some states (Czechoslovakia, Rumania and the Soviet Union itself were particularly strict) foreigners were only permitted to use certain specific 'tourist' hotels, restaurants and shops. These were generally better in terms of quality than those available to the locals but carried the huge disadvantage that everything had to be paid for in dollars. They were also indescribably boring; totally lacking local colour or any hint of a market or trading atmosphere.

In the Soviet block at this time camping brought with it its own characteristic state oversight. For a start camping was only permitted at a handful of official sites, located for the most part adjacent to, or within the grounds of, a state-run tourist hotel. Some were pretty good in terms of facilities, but petty rules and heavy-handed regulation meant that *dull and drab* would usually be a fair summary for what was experienced. The most irritating restriction of all was that in most of the Eastern Bloc states a campsite stay had to be pre-booked and paid for several months in advance, making a flexible itinerary virtually impossible. On the other hand, these state-inspired limitations, with due care, could be successfully challenged, defied or cheerfully ignored and a huge amount of fun and adventure enjoyed in so doing.

Rumanians in the 1980s were, perhaps with only the Albanians excepted, the most downtrodden of all the peoples of socialist Europe and most were scared to be seen even talking to a foreigner let alone permitting a busload of them to camp in their field or garden. The trick, therefore, was to find a bit of scrub or forest, discretely off the beaten track, but with road access. The disused gravel quarry we spotted some thirty or forty miles beyond Oradea seemed ideal. Grassy and dotted with shady willows, it was divided by a merrily babbling stream that flowed beneath a rustic wooden bridge. Approaching cautiously along the roughish track which had brought us from the main road, I'd had doubts about the bridge and – just in case the worst should happen – had first disgorged my passengers. Despite much creaking and groaning from ancient timbers, all went well and when I parked up a few yards on, I noted with satisfaction that we were now conveniently invisible from the main road.

By now the boys were superb campers and, without a single order or instruction either from me or from Roy, they had tents erected and a meal underway in next to no time. It was a lovely calm and warm evening with a cheerful, red-streaked sky. Close at hand the big gas stove hissed its culinary promise, birds twittered as they made ready for the night and the stream gurgled pleasantly. In the distance the rumble of a diesel freight train making its way among the wooded hills seemed somehow to give a final touch of homely reassurance. It was at that precise moment I realised we were being watched.

Two small boys and two men of gypsy appearance were standing stock-still under a **willow** tree about twenty yards away. The boys had fishing roads in their hands.

"Roy, we've been rumbled."

"Eh?"

I pointed. "Over there…"

"I see."

"I think it's just curiosity but…" An idea had suddenly struck me. "Is Tom Cairns occupied?"

"Not specially. I think. Why?"

"He's mad keen on fishing, isn't he? Hasn't he brought a rod with him? Why not get him and another lad to take the rod over and ask about fishing? You never know, it might sort of help relations."

Tom, at twelve, was our youngest adventurer and a game enough lad to boot and in no time at all was ready with a pal to perform his diplomatic mission.

"Where are they, sir?" he asked as he came up to me complete with rod and basket.

"Over there by that tr…goodness, they've gone!"

They really had and, though I kept a weather eye open through our meal and as we closed down for the night. It appeared they'd left us for good. By the time I did my final round of the camp, checking all was well and that things of value had been locked away, it was properly nighttime with a clear star-lit sky and rising moon. Now and then an owl hooted and occasionally in the distance a dog barked. I picked up my toothbrush and paste and went down to the stream, walking along the bank in the darkness searching for a suitable spot. A couple of humpy rocks suggested likely access and I stepped carefully onto them. To say these rocks failed my expectations would grossly understate the shock they gave me. The 'rocks' not only moved, as wobbly rocks can, but these were also warm and soft to my clumsy touch. They also yelped, for I had stepped on the two boy-fishermen.

My ability to apologise in Rumanian, I need hardly add, was next to nil and was further diminished by the fraught circumstances. Despite a pounding heart and laboured breathing, I did the best I could, but I have seldom felt more ridiculous or incoherent. Rumanian youth must be made of sterner stuff: They were still there fishing when I woke early the next morning. As our camp came slowly to life, the fisher-boys came over to watch our doings. And their faces said it all.

Time and time again when camping in remote places populated by poor and backward communities, I've seen the self-same blend of wonder and incomprehension right now marking the expressions worn by these two fisher boys. "Here are these foreigners," the local folk on these occasions were surely saying to themselves, "all of them rich beyond our dreams yet living by choice like homeless vagabonds. Whilst we have to slave and struggle for years in backbreaking labour to afford ourselves some dank hovel, these mad foreigners, who everybody knows have mansions with bathrooms and God knows what other luxuries and marvels, are washing themselves in a stream!"

"For Heaven's sake stop poking that camera at them all the time," I snapped at one of our boys with uncalled for irritation. "You'd do better offering them something to eat, considering they've been up all night."

"OK sir," he said with a cheeriness that put my mood to shame.

I doubt if the two Rumanian boys had ever seen such a breakfast, let along eaten one. And when they scampered off moments later with a packet of McVitie's chocolate digestives lying with the five small fishes they'd caught overnight in their basket, my world somehow seemed just a wee bit better.

"Sir, have I got time to fish just a bit?"

"Well not really, Tom…well…" I hesitated, not wanting to sound unreasonable, "Oh sir! You see, sir, those boys told us where's a good spot."

Flipping marvellous! Last night I had trampled on them and all but knocked them into the water and wasn't able to make a decent apology; and yet here is young Tom able to get detailed fishing information out of them. Someone up there, I felt, was running an anti-adult world.

"OK," I muttered resignedly, "you can have about half an hour if that's any good."

Ten minutes later a skinny woman turned up with a child in her arms and two very dirty toddlers clutching her grubby ankle-length skirt. There was no beating about the bush: she came directly into our midst holding out a rag bundle in her spare hand.

The rags contained half a dozen tiny hens' eggs. She said not a word but made a mournful whining noise and we could all see she was in a state of abject fear. I didn't want the eggs so there was no sense in trying to do a deal and I simply pressed a small wad of Rumanian money into her palm and took the eggs. She fumbled with the money and I think she was about to hand some of it back when her roving, anxious eyes suddenly rounded into a fixed gaze. I glanced behind to see what had caught her attention. A police jeep was slowly coming up the track from the main road but by the time I'd turned again, the woman, now carrying two children, with the third scampering beside her, was disappearing into the trees.

In many ways the Rumanian countryside was enchantingly beautiful, especially in the valleys of the Carpathian Mountains, but everywhere we turned there was terrible poverty and evidence of the corroding hand of the Ceausescu regime. As we passed through age-old rustic settlements, we were intrigued by the richly carved eaves and doorways of the cottages, a characteristic feature of rural Rumania, but, at the same time sad and horrified by the deliberate and contemptuous intrusion of hideous concrete pylons erected by the state electricity authorities. Captivating little wooden churches, lovingly preserved unchanged for centuries, were similarly blighted by having concrete bus shelters of appalling crudity built right next to them. All these shocking measures were part of a deliberate policy by the Ceausescu regime of destroying village life and traditions so that the population would have no choice but to accept the new 'Collective Communities', built and designed to enable even greater regime control over the population. It was surely a great pity when Ceausescu and his cronies got their comeuppance in the 1989 overthrow of the regime, that Rumania's ancient hero, Vlad the Impaler, was no longer around to practise his remarkable hobby.

By the close of our first full day's travel in Rumania we had only spent about a third of the currency we'd been obliged to convert. Apart from the *lei* we'd given to the peasant woman, all the rest of our spend had been on amazingly cheap, though surprisingly hard to find, petrol. Quite simply, in Ceausescu's socialist paradise there was virtually nothing in what few shops there were that any sane Westerner would want to buy. In one town we passed through we decided, largely just for the experience, to sample the so-called supermarket. There were no trolleys or wire baskets and clearly, (as in the Soviet Union at the same period), you were expected to bring your own bags and these were searched as we entered by a generously proportioned, but determinedly unsmiling, matron figure. She was, I recall, the only cuddly-shaped person we came across in that land of gaunt and dispirited souls. The walls and some of the display counters of this particular People's Emporium had once been surfaced with plain white tiles – presumably as a concession to the notion of hygiene – but at least a third of them were now cracked or missing. Even those which had so far managed to remain in position had clearly been slapped on without the slightest effort to achieve a neat and proper job. Indeed, the appalling crudity and scandalous quality of workmanship in virtually every post-war structure in Rumania was probably, for me, the single most remembered feature of the country.

The monotony of such tiles as managed to stay adhered to the walls was to a certain extent relieved by streaks of slimy green mould marking places where, over the years, the roof had been leaking. Dense clusters of flies, camped out on the many pools of undetermined gunge, added their own touch to the milieu of this state retail outlet. The floor appeared to be of simple rough concrete but in places it was not easy to be sure owing to an overlay of flattened cartons, blooded sawdust and the detritus of stock long since sold. Naked bulbs and flickering fluorescents provided just enough light to navigate by and to determine the general character of the stock.

There were but two categories of foodstuff on sale. Several large bins made of galvanised wire contained ample supplies of bread, though choice appeared limited to a standard unwrapped loaf of breeze-block proportions. I noticed that a piece of tarpaulin had been placed by the shop's obviously assiduous management over a bin sited where the roof seemed particularly prone to rainwater ingress. The second product was also stocked in some quantity but its nature at first had us baffled. Large glass jars filled with soggy wadges of dark-green minced up leaves were on sale. Row upon row of them filled a dozen or more shelves. My pocket Rumanian-English dictionary, hastily fetched from the bus, revealed the mystery product to be bottled spinach. It would be hard to envisage a more repulsive-looking foodstuff – 'just like horse vomit' was the charming description of the product by Dave Armstrong and, as a farmer's son, I suppose his view carried clout. At all events I purchased a bottle as a keepsake and it stands to this day on a shelf in my garage alongside my GUNK and Holt's radiator sludge remover. Although ninety percent of the shelves were bare at the time of our visit, we later discovered that if you were serious about your food shopping in Ceausescu's Rumania you had to get up at the crack of dawn and then queue for the modest quantities of onions, flour, eggs and cooking oil that were sometimes available when the shop first opened.

A little later, as I handed the driving over to Roy during our passage through the seventh police checkpoint since crossing the frontier, I thought it a good moment to discuss our plans for the next section of our journey.

"I've been thinking, Roy, that it will make more sense if we leave Bucharest out of the route and instead go to Bulgaria by cutting through Yugoslavia."

"Well, that Dutch lorry driver wasn't what I'd call encouraging about the delays on the Danube crossing point."

"Exactly. There's a second reason though. Bucharest means at least another day, possibly two and that'll involve converting still more dollars into the Micky Mouse stuff. Damn it, Roy, so far we haven't even managed to spend what Rumanian we've already got."

"True, but aren't you forgetting that it will take about a day to get from here to Yugoslavia?"

"No, Roy. What I have in mind is to buy dinner in some half-decent hotel – supposing there is such a thing in this country – and then drive on all through the night, hopefully reaching the Yugoslav border before it becomes necessary to convert more dollars. Not cooking will save two or more hours and buying dinner should just about mop up our stock of this rubbish money."

The Hydro Hotel near Râmnicu Vâlcea was a tall, impressively sited building overlooking a tree-filled gorge. The dozen cars in the large car park seemed a good deal smarter than the decrepit specimens generally encountered on Rumanian roads. I was encouraged.

"The bod in the petrol place could be right," said Roy, scanning the scene as we disembarked the boys and the 'security gang' (Adrian Meynell and Dave Armstrong) commenced their vital locking-up routine – windows shut and all catches secure, steering lock in place, doors locked, roof rack tarpaulin tight with elastic rope made fast and all trailer padlocks on and closed. We had gone to some trouble to locate this place, most towns and villages in Ceausescu's Rumania lacking anything better than a run-down wine bar. A succession of enquiries had yielded little more than shrugged shoulders or blank stares. Then, just as despair was beginning to raise its head, a lounger at a petrol station volunteered information about an "'otel very OK", the man having caught on to the fact that we weren't at all interested in the characterless official 'tourist hotels'.

First impressions in the entrance foyer were tolerably encouraging and, yes, the clearly astonished receptionist admitted, the restaurant could accommodate a party of thirteen diners. At a quick roadside halt a mile or so before reaching the hotel I had obliged the boys to wash in a stream and put on clean shirts and it was satisfying to note that the quality of the place was making sense of my unpopular demand. As with most state enterprises in Eastern Europe, the restaurant was hugely overmanned, there being seven or eight waiters for the handful of tables in use. The décor was what I would term 'heavy Soviet' – elaborate (but very dusty) tasselled lampshades in deep red velvet; several sets of matching plush velvet curtains capped by fussy pelmets; large, tall-backed dining chairs assembled from a jungle of elaborately turned spindles and finials; the tables bearing droopy folds of grubby off-white lace.

The large, high-ceilinged room appeared to have far more curtains than a reasonable provision of doors and windows should command and, Rumania being Rumania, I half-seriously half-suspected some of them might be used as hiding places for agents of the *Securitate,* the regime's all-pervasive secret police. Having jocularly voiced my suspicions, Phil Cairns, our on-board mischief maker, with some talent for acting, offered to take a peep behind each curtain and, rather irresponsibly, I allowed him to go ahead. Phil was a born mimic and his performance was not only hilarious, but quite transparent in its political focus.

Rumania may be a Latin country in language and in some aspects of its culture but under Nicolae Ceausescu Latin *joie de vivre* was clearly out of fashion and, after an unthinking little chuckle here and there among our fellow diners, a portentous silence quickly enveloped the room. Not really surprising, I suppose, given that a smile in the wrong circumstances could cost you your liberty in Rumania's socialist paradise.

It is well that the Trades Description Act does not apply in Rumania. The menu had promised steak but what we got were small sausages. The wine, however, was wine and not too bad at that but it was the dessert that upset the stately routine of the establishment. Apple and prune(?) pie had arrived but neither custard nor cream, it seemed, was available to temper the leathery texture of the pastry. A shame, for sitting in our minibus were several tins of Carnation evaporated milk.

"Craig," I said, passing him the keys of the bus, "be a good fellow and go and fetch a couple of tins of Carnation. Oh, and bring a screwdriver."

"Two Carnation," he called minutes later, placing the tins on the table beside me. "I couldn't see a screwdriver, though, sir."

"Never mind. I'll ask the waiter to open them."

When the waiter returned, he was followed by a rather distinguished-looking character in a grey suit, who turned out to be the hotel manager. The tins, I noticed, had been opened, which rather opposed my first thought – that I was about to be rebuked for importing our own food into the restaurant. As the boys began sharing round the milk, the manager came close to my chair and, after a slight bow, said with polished grace: "This excellent cream, sir, is it possible you have another tin that you would permit me to purchase?"

I must have spent an age staring at him open-mouthed as I strove to adjust my thoughts to this unexpected turn. Adrian was as quick as I was slow.

"We have at least a couple of dozen," he boomed. "What does a box hold? Forty-eight isn't it?"

"A b–b–box! Believe me, sir, I would be very interested…" So, I noticed, were people at some of the other tables. The manager glanced nervously round the room.

"For goodness' sake, Adrian," I hissed, "pipe down and leave it to me."

After anxiously running his tongue over his lips, the manager explained in quiet conspiratorial tones that real cream was virtually unobtainable in Rumania and even mere milk was restricted to families with infants. Everyone else in this land of broad and lush pastures was expected to make do with powdered milk, but to make matters still worse, this was seemingly a product of abysmal quality. The manager had closed his eyes and shuddered as he mentioned it! I had no objection to selling a few cans – which we could easily replace in Istanbul – but the manager wanted to pay in *lei* whereas I was only willing to accept dollars. Honour was in the end satisfied at ten tins for a fifty percent discount on the meal with cups of free *nes* – Rumanian instant coffee – thrown in.

If the manager thought his low-voiced negotiations would escape the notice of his other guests, then he was wrong. As we filed out to the bus, a line of eager traders followed and closed round the bus in an expectant semi-circle. Had we, by any chance, any spare soap? Detergent – *Pearseel* – would be equally desirable. Shampoo? Oh wonderful! The boys entered into the spirit of this incipient Rumanian capitalism with gusto and had to be restrained from selling off their entire stock of toiletries. In exchange we acquired two or three bottles of Rumanian wine and one of *Tuica* – a mouth-searing national spirit distilled from plums. Looking back at the whole business of our trading experience at the Hydro Hotel, it is striking to note that all our 'customers' must have been members of the governing elite to have been dining in such a hotel in the first place. So much for the reality of equality in socialist Rumania!

I took over the driving from Roy in the cold grey light of dawn. The changeover had broken the fretful slumbers of some of the contorted, limb-entwined humanity in the rear.

"Where are we?"

"Take your sodding foot off my face!"

"Oh God...what's the time?"

The bus smelt like a gorilla's armpit and I wound down my window as we picked up speed, ignoring someone's mumbled protest. It wasn't yet 5 o'clock, yet people were already beginning the day's drudgery. We passed several mule carts – long, narrow four-wheeled affairs like sagging-in-the-middle open coffins – generally trundling along with a whole family aboard, pitch forks aloft, heading for work in the fields where the harvest would be got in largely by hand. None carried lights. And in the large grey fields, hundreds of grey Lowry men were bending and stooping among horse-drawn carts already piled high with hay and straw.

"You know what," said Roy, trying to stifle a huge yawn. "This journey through Rumania will have inoculated these lads of ours against communism for life. Just look at those poor devils over there. It's like a scene from the Middle Ages."

"Sir," called out Adrian from somewhere in nether regions of the bus. "Would you say Karl Marx was a great philosopher?"

"Goodness Adrian, what a question at five in the morning!"

"I don't know anything about philosophy and stuff," chipped in Craig in dry, grumpy tones, "but I'll tell you one thing. It takes only half an hour in Rumania to realise old Marxy-boy was a God-awful economist."

Chapter 6

Constantinople, Byzantium, Istanbul or even Miklagard; call it what you will, is one of the most thrilling cities on earth. Where else has served as the capital of two very different but equally great and enduring empires? What other city stands astride two continents? Has any other city been the seat of supreme power for both Christianity and Islam, the world's two leading religions? For twenty-seven centuries this greatest of metropolises, straddling the confluences of the Golden Horn and the Bosporus, has been a palimpsest of succeeding civilisations. It is still today the place where in every sense and nuance, East meets West. We arrived there on Sunday 29th of July.

Nothing very exceptional had marked the days between our thankful dawn exit from Rumania on July 26th and our expectant, excited and starry-eyed entry to Istanbul three days later. In 1984 Yugoslavia was still enjoying the stability established during the Tito years though the rumblings of destructive nationalism, which commenced soon after the great man's death in 1980, were already emerging in the province of Kosovo. However, our route down the country's south-eastern border zone occasioned nothing worse than stretches of rough unpaved road and almost before we knew it, we found ourselves in the queue of buses and trucks lined up at the

Bulgarian frontier.

During the early eighties Bulgaria bore the reputation of being one of the most slavish of the satellites of the Soviet Union. This close affinity is easily explained. In 1878 it was Russia who liberated the Bulgars from their Ottoman oppressors and in 1944 the favour was repeated when the Soviets kicked out the German Nazis.

Furthermore, Russia and Bulgaria share a common heritage in their strong ties with the faith of the Orthodox Church and in their use of the Cyrillic alphabet for their closely related languages. The border formalities were not too bad though initially we found it confusing that to Bulgarians a nod means 'no' and a side-to-side movement of the head indicates 'yes'! We were all given what the border militia termed a *carte statistique.*

The idea, a bulky, freely perspiring militia policeman told us, was that at each hotel, hostel, or campsite where we spent a night, the receptionist would stamp the card. He was quite a cheerful fellow and, punctuating his efforts at English with belly-shaking chuckles, strongly advised us not to forget. People trying to leave the country with an incomplete card, he laughingly explained, would get 'a big *smetkata*' – a big bill or fine! Clearly the real purpose of the card was to prevent foreign visitors staying in private houses, this being expressly forbidden as the regime was anxious to minimise exposure of its citizens to Western ways. As we had had it in mind to spend our night in Bulgaria simply camped in some quiet rural spot, this unexpected piece of red tape was bad news.

Although graced by a few pleasant tree-lined boulevards, overall, there is not a great deal to detain a traveller in Sofia, Bulgaria's capital. For this, History is largely to blame. To start with, during the long centuries of rule by the Ottoman Turks, which as just mentioned did not end until 1878, by decree no building was allowed to exceed the height of a man riding on horseback. This bizarre law was devised to stymie any possible Bulgarian insurrection taking advantage of the old city's web of narrow, twisting streets and dark, rancorous alleyways. Although in some cases the law was ingeniously circumvented by sinking buildings below ground level, by and large its effect has been to deprive Sofia of any significant architectural heritage. Second, making the architectural scene bleaker still, buildings destroyed during the Second World War were replaced by the usual hideous, ill-built, grey, characterless blocks that the Soviets so enthusiastically favoured.

Plovdiv, just over one hundred miles further on and Bulgaria's second city, was altogether more interesting and we spend several hours there exploring the Old Town where, among several notable sights, there are the remains of a Roman amphitheatre. Just outside Plovdiv we spotted an official camping site, largely populated by the extraordinary tiny caravans which were a feature of the Communist Balkan states.

Perhaps their size bore a relationship to the pulling powers of the ubiquitous 'Trabi', but at six or seven foot in length and their other dimensions in proportion, they were certainly the Wendy houses of the caravan world.

We elected to take our supper in the site's open air '*pectopa*' and at the coffee stage we were given, courtesy of Phil and Slackie, a portrayal of the contortions a fat lady and her husband might be supposed to endure whilst undressing and preparing for bed in such a caravan. I have to concede their performance was top rate and it had all of us – and quite a few Bulgarians too – in stiches.

Instead of staying on the site overnight I wanted to press on towards Svilengrad, the border town on the Turkish frontier, so as to be well placed for an early crossing before long queues had built up. But what about the dreaded *cartes statistiques?* Well, the 'pectopah' manageress had been pretty friendly and had shown great interest in the circumstances of our journey so I wondered if she might be willing to stamp our document when I paid for the meal. It seemed worth a try.

"Oh," she said when I presented it, "that gets stamped tomorrow morning."

"Can't you do it now to save time" I countered, putting on what I hoped would be an encouraging smile. At first, she scowled and repeated her 'wait until tomorrow' message but my disappointment must have shown for she suddenly shrugged her shoulders, snatched the proffered document, stamped it and impatiently gave it back to me almost as if I were a pestering child.

"Are you not also paying for the camping now as well, instead of in the morning?" she then asked.

"Er…no."

Staring at me in some suspicion, I think she was about to question me further when, luckily, she was called by one of her staff. I slipped quietly out of her office. Moments later, without noise or fuss, I got everybody aboard the bus, started up and gently stole away into the night.

It was well after eleven when I cautiously eased the bus and trailer off the main road and nosed my way, headlights extinguished, in bright moonlight down a farm track. After two hundred or so yards of growling progress I stopped to let Roy and Dave Armstrong begin on foot a silent reconnaissance of our immediate neighbourhood.

"Just the ticket," said Roy, abruptly reappearing as a black form some minutes later. "Follow and I'll help you park up. It's a few yards off the track but solid all the way."

"Listen chaps," I urged in no more than a loud whisper, facing round towards the rear of the bus. "We're going to pass the night right here. We are in the middle of some sort of farm so there must be no noise at all. The police could be really difficult if they caught us. So, no talking, no slamming of doors and no torches."

The atmosphere in the bus had become charged. The feeling of adventure was palpable. Faces were only half-recognisable in the moon-sourced glimmer, but I was looking at a circle of bright, eager eyes.

"The night is warm," I continued. "No tents. The roof boys will throw down your sleeping bags and karrimats. Any questions?"

"To clean our tee—"

"In the morning," I hissed quickly, anxious to forestall the jeers likely after such a naff question.

"Right. You've got five minutes to settle down."

They did a good job and I don't think trained soldiers would have been significantly better. Exactly five minutes later I performed my little round to make sure everyone was OK.

"Sir, what's that smell?" whispered Tom Cairns as I picked my way past his sleeping bag. I sniffed and then walked over to the crop growing beyond the trees which circled our little grassy space.

"Tobacco plants, Tom."

"Quite a nice smell, sir."

"I think I'd like to give tobacco a try."

I kicked the form in the sleeping bag with measured significant force. "Sweet dreams, Tom."

We woke at about six-thirty to the throbbing rumble of a tractor and trailer carrying a posse of farm workers to their labours. Our bus with its farrow of somnolent shapes littered around it attracted pointed arms and curious glances but no sign of disapproval so I felt we could risk breakfast. Eight-thirty saw us back on the main road without let or hindrance and shortly afterwards we were in the tangle of parked trucks and buses which marked the frontier with Turkey. Judging from the thicket of onlookers we attracted and from the questions thrown at us from other drivers, a 'GB' plate here was something of a rarity. Before I had even worked out where we were supposed to go, a white-coated official had come up to my window and asked for our passports. According to a shirtless Turkish truck driver, built like a wrestler and looking like one with his shaven head and tooled and studded black leather breeches, this was a good sign and meant we were likely to be free to cross over to Turkey (and be ready to face a repeat of the process) within a couple of hours. Roy and I tried to relax patiently in the hot sunshine whilst keeping an eye on the bus as well as the goings on of

50

our gang. The latter, wandering about in twos and threes, were busy drinking in the bustle and colourful chaos of the scene.

Those whose experience of land frontiers is confined to the slick efficiency and respectful courtesies of Dover-Calais or like crossing points within Western Europe, can have little conception of the trials and frustrations that in Soviet times were normal at a frontier like Svilengrad. For starters, on both sides of the divide most officials were disorganised, work-shy and capricious. They also displayed a marked penchant for allowing favoured friends to queue jump. With the Communists in particular, any sense of order or discipline went hand in hand with a parallel air of corruption and oppression. The Turkish speciality appeared to be sheer chaos; chaos fuelled in large part by an army of pestering street traders and general hangers-on.

Many Turkish officials had neither uniform nor badge. On one occasion I had handed over the vehicle's papers in response to a call and an outstretched hand only to discover I'd given them to a truck driver simply curious to see what British documents looked like! On the Turkish side waiting vehicles more or less parked where they pleased and it was far from clear which were waiting to enter Turkey and which were crossing to Bulgaria. In short, keeping tabs on documents, possessions and pupils was something of a nightmare.

We camped the night of the twenty-fourth in a sunflower field within sight and sound of Istanbul's Ataturk airport. It was strangely exciting lying there on the threshold of a city that had been our destination over weeks of travel. Anticipation was enhanced and imagination flourished. Here, outside walls that had seen off a hundred sieges, perhaps we'd chanced to lie exactly where, in some century long gone, warlike men had also set their camp.

East ran the road next morning and dead ahead was the giant red-gold sun rising in the sky and filling the windscreen more and more until it seemed we must be travelling in a spaceship towards a great red planet. And all the while to the left and right of us the sprawling scruffy suburbs of Istanbul, falsely beautiful in the weird pearl-pink iridescence of the eastern dawn. Straight ahead were the city's great walls and at the Edirne Gate the tidal surge of rush hour traffic swept us into the heaving, vibrant city.

Foreseeing likely difficulty in finding secure camping anywhere near the centre of such a vast ocean of urbanisation, I had pre-booked some rooms in the Hotel Toro, a recommended 'cheapo' hidden in a leafy corner a dozen or so blocks from the historic heart of the city. Yet my foresight availed me nothing for the crafty old devil who owned the place had double-booked the accommodation and we arrived to find he had given 'our' rooms to some young Australians. His bogus excuse was to claim we had not arrived when expected but, bluntly told that midmorning was hardly late in the day for claiming hotel rooms, he changed tack and blamed the mix-up on his 'boy'! The man was the personification of the oily oriental of cheap fiction. There was the leering, the ingratiating smile; the dirty suit and excess of flashy rings; the flabbiness and sallow skin. Clearly, he was as much a stranger to exercise, fresh air and daylight as he was to honest dealing. I had just rejected his offer to "send my boy to fix you up at another hotel very clean and not very far" when some of my own fellows burst into the entrance foyer carrying their rucksacks and other luggage.

"Doesn't look too bad, sir," exclaimed Alan Beattie breezily. "Which floor are we on?"

"Will it be two to a room, sir?" spluttered James Gill, letting his rucksack fall unchecked to crash against a large bronze standard lamp which I only just managed to save from toppling over.

"Do watch what you're doing! And who told you to come in anyway? I thought I said to wait in the bus."

"Mr Woodforde sent us, sir. There's lots of kids and other guys pestering us wanting to carry stuff and Mr Woodforde thought we'd better start…"

There was another crash and two more heavily laden boys parachuted into the foyer.

"Hang on chaps!" I called, holding my hand up arrestingly. "There's a problem and it's not certain we'll be staying in this hote…"

I'd stopped because an interesting idea, triggered by the look on the old Turk's face as the second pair of boys carelessly dumped their loads onto one of the foyer sofas, had just crossed my mind.

"On the floor, boys," I groaned, putting on a pained expression, "not on the furniture! What uncivilised hooligans you are!"

They both mumbled an apology and made to move their stuff.

"Leave it now, it's there. But look, go and tell Mr Woodforde to keep sending stuff. The more the better."

In very little time, all the boys, saving a couple left outside to guard the bus, were sprawled about the foyer; noisy and not quite certain what was expected of them, but sporting a vaguely threatening air like rough cowboys in a smart saloon. Heaps of our luggage and belongings were strewn all over the place, effectively demonstrating the permanence of our arrival.

"That seems very reasonable," I concluded some minutes later, nodding to the proprietor. "So, we get the use of the upstairs sitting room as a place to lock up our bags and so on, we can go to whatever bathrooms there are on any of the floors and we employ the roof garden with some rugs and mattresses for sleeping. And all at one dollar each person each night?"

"But no food," he added anxiously. "No, no food."

The fellow looked relieved and then nodded his agreement just as Roy came up

"Is something wrong?"

"On the contrary, Roy, all is very well. Thanks to the disturbing presence in his smart foyer of these unprepossessing youths of ours, not to mention their untidy possessions, this excellent proprietor has just given us a sevenfold reduction in the tariff, subject only to a small drop in the grade of room."

Chapter 7

The throbbing, intoxicating pulse of Istanbul entered our veins the second we stepped out into the clammy hot streets and, although we were still in the European sector of the city, the oriental character of the traffic was at once apparent. Many will infer from this that I mean the traffic was chaotic and lawless and that drivers displayed no respect whatever towards cyclists and pedestrians. In fact, I don't mean that at all. From Cairo to Calcutta and anywhere between, when you stand back and study the traffic of great oriental cities and try to 'read' it with an open mind, you begin to see that there certainly are rules, though most are very different from ours. Primarily they are informal and 'understood' rather than the product of legislation and regulation. One might describe them as 'organic'. And often they're very subtle too and call for meaningful eye contact with other drivers; also, for a degree of second- guessing and alert reaction which is foreign to our pampered home territory experience. I have to confess I enjoy the challenge of driving in the Middle East and in Asia.

Istanbul, with its teeming population and its profusion of tangled tenements and nameless alleyways lying cheek by jowl with its best thoroughfares, raised stark issues with respect to the safety and well-being of the boys in my charge. I am afraid I have little patience with today's fashion for believing that when anything unfortunate happens, someone must be found upon whom to pin blame and from whom ambulance chasing lawyers can wring compensation. The result is a cover-my-back culture of daft and mean-spirited restrictions dishonestly labelled 'health and safety'. The honest fact is that most children – and healthy boys in particular – require a measure of risk in their lives. If we so regulate home and school that risk is effectively eliminated, then watch out, for our children will soon be inventing their own. It is the bored children of a dysfunctional society who play 'chicken' on railway lines.

The solution, as ever, lies not in totality but in a common-sense balance. Children need busy, well-ordered regimes in which there is a place for just enough risk to learn about life and to satisfy their innate spirit of adventure. Was not the adventure of it the essential justification for this overland journey to

India? Yet the very word *adventure,* as the dictionary tells us, is an 'enterprise of uncertain outcome'! So where is the balance to be struck? Surely, as so often is the case, the traditional English formula provides the best answer – or it would if only must-be-seen-to-be-doing-something politicians would leave it alone. The formula is the legal concept of 'in loco parentis', whereby the teacher is required to act on behalf of the parent *in the manner of* a caring parent. Now what caring parent would wish to see his child exposed to serious risk? On the other hand, what caring parent – mindful of the child's true needs would deny the child a spot of adventure appropriate to age, personality and ability?

In practice, of course, it is all down to judgement and it cannot be denied that Istanbul is a huge city with its fair share of dangerous and dubious neighbourhoods. Yet, as such cities go, in the 1980s it was a pretty safe place and, in my book, this meant that it was not only acceptable, but in fact very desirable that the boys should be given a certain degree of freedom there. Freedom to explore it on their own and to 'do their own thing'. Freedom even to get lost in a minor way or run into small problems; thereby gaining experience and having the fun of sorting themselves out. Not of course alone, but in twos or threes and always within a fairly tight timeframe.

I knew that once the boys had tasted the Kapali Carsi. Istanbul's enormous world-famous covered bazaar, they would be reluctant to spend time anywhere else so our first two days in Istanbul were largely given over to visiting the great mosques and similar must-see places. The Hagia Sophia (St Sophia's), now a museum, stands today in glorious witness to the many achievements of the Emperor Justinian I (527-565), whose entire reign was given over to the Herculean task of re-establishing the majestic authority and ancient boundaries of the Roman Empire. He and his principal commander, the eunuch Belisarius, came surprisingly close to success. In many ways this church of the 'divine wisdom' is Christendom's greatest edifice and the building we see today is essentially the building Justinian left to us. It is sobering to recall that St Sophia's had been standing more than half a millennium before the building of Durham cathedral, sometimes suggested as England's greatest medieval church, had even begun. When the Byzantine Roman Empire ended on the capture of Constantinople by the Ottoman Turks in 1453, St Sophia's became a mosque, its Romano-Christian architectural form ironically setting the style for many of Islam's most cherished buildings. It takes several hours to do full justice to this enormous church and when, at last, we emerged into the afternoon sunshine, immediate recourse to a *doner kebabi* stall was needed to stave off mutiny. Next it was down to the Galata bridge to take in the tumultuous sights and scenes of the waterfront where the Golden Horn, alas now something of a reeking sewer, joins the Bosporus. The southward view from this bridge forms one of Istanbul's most characteristic vistas: A hill dominated by the domes and minarets of the Yeni Cami (New Mosque). All around it are picturesque, cobbled alleys where you can still find the arcaded courtyards of ancient *caravanserais* – the Ottoman period equivalent of today's motel. There are also numerous markets and bazaars, including the famous Spice Bazaar. In late Byzantine times this area was the 'foreign quarter' and home to the merchant strongholds of various powerful Italian city-states. One of their structures, the Galata Tower (Tower of Christ), built in 1348, still stands as a major landmark. Its penultimate floor, almost 200-feet above the street, is now a restaurant where there is a floor show of 'traditional' belly dancing. But, maybe not as traditional as all that for the dancing girls were German, not Turkish. And how do I know this?

Well, because we ended our first day in Istanbul by treating ourselves to dinner in the tower's restaurant and one of our sharp-eared German-learning GCSE boys happened to hear a couple of the dancers conversing off-stage in the tongue of the fatherland. Due enquiry into this apparent cultural anomaly then produced an explanation by our waiter of the factors influencing the employment of belly dancers, followed by the heady bonus of a word or two in German with some of the delectable frauleins as they rested between dances perched on the laps of blushing young Englanders. At all events, the boys' enthusiasm for speaking German appeared to have undergone a remarkable improvement since our little contretemps in the Munich car park.

We began our second day by proceeding to the Blue Mosque (the mosque of Sultan Ahmet I), started in 1609 and finished in 1617. It is said that Ahmet was in such a hurry to see his new mosque finished that he often slipped out of his palace in disguise to work on the building himself. He had good reason to be impatient for, within a year of its completion, he was dead. This mosque, with its elegant cascades of domes and six slender minarets is one of Istanbul's most splendid sights. The Park in front of this mosque is laid out on the site of the ancient Roman Hippodrome with the streets around its periphery following the original racetrack. Built around AD 200 by the Emperor Septimius Severus, the Hippodrome was the focus of Byzantium's turbulent street politics and served as its killing field in 532 when Justinian trapped and slaughtered 30,000 rebels during a major revolt against his rule. The area is now

Istanbul's most touristy spot and the parking place of dozens of Pullman buses that disgracefully foul the air with their continually running engines – kept going just so their spoilt passengers can return to air-conditioned self-indulgence. This is also a much-favoured place for gypsies with performing bears and for pushy street traders of all descriptions. It was here, among the street traders and tourist buses that the death toll for the Hippodrome came close to claiming victim number thirty thousand and one.

In my experience most teenage boys entertain two great vanities. The first is that they are ordained by nature to be expert car drivers; flair and panache being innate gifts denied their mothers and sisters and long since atrophied in their fathers. The second is that their hard-headed masculine outlook will ensure they always know a bargain when they see one. Sky high insurance premiums for young male drivers give the lie to the first vanity; a minibus full of treasured designed-for-suckers souvenirs amply illustrated the sad self-deception of the second. And, despite all my careful warnings, one of our parties emerged with pride from beating down a street trader's initial fifty-pound price tag for a 'genuine' Rolex to something much more reasonable! Another was sufficiently persistent to acquire three *genuine* Lacoste shirts for a mere five pounds apiece. Ah well, I suppose the bottom line was that the game was enjoyed in true Olympic spirit: the honour being in taking part in bargaining rather than in emerging financially victorious.

Such was the general picture, but one or two boys were made of sterner stuff. David Tite's extrovert streetwise temperament, for example, found music for his soul in Istanbul's oriental trading practices and he was determined to make his mark. The Hippodrome area was especially favoured by the many sellers of wooden pipes and flutes which, they glibly assure anybody who'll listen, are *bona fide* handmade instruments, as used by shepherds in the remote Anatolian highlands. Adrian, who was about grade 5 on the recorder, managed to wring a recognisable melody from a gaudily painted example and thereupon decided upon purchase. Thus encouraged, a couple of other boys then did likewise. Somehow or other, David Tite was able to talk his trader into letting him have a flute for about half the price Adrian had paid and this success planted a novel idea in David's mind. What price, he asked, if he were to buy a round dozen? The trader was unable to hide his surprise. A lifetime's experience had taught him tourists could easily be wheedled into paying well over the odds for a single flute, but until then he had never had anyone interested in buying by the dozen. A final skirmish and David had got himself twelve very cheap flutes.

"Slackie's finally flipped," Adrian excitedly informed a couple of friends minutes later. "He's just bought about twenty flutes and says he's going to sell them to tourists as they come off the buses."

I'm told Adrian's news was received with some scepticism until David's portly figure was seen heading purposefully past the famous Serpent Column towards the parked-up tourist coaches. Incredibly, it seems he was largely successful. Too successful!

Needless to say, neither I nor Roy knew anything of David's pioneering commercial venture. We had given the boys two hours to look round on their own and had arranged to meet again at midday when we were all due to tour the Blue Mosque. At about ten to twelve David appeared at our agreed rendezvous at the bottom of the steps leading up to the mosque's main entrance. He was flushed and dishevelled and looked as if he'd been in a fight.

"Can I go straight into the mosque, sir, without waiting for the others?"

"Why David, whatever is the matter?"

"Nothing sir. I…I'm hot, that's all and it will be cooler inside."

It was obvious his answer was a half-truth at best and my suspicions were increased by his early return. David's style was to arrive, well-armed with excuses, at the very last minute.

"It would be better to wait so that we can all go in together."

"Oh sir, *please* can't I go in now?" As he pleaded, he was glancing anxiously all about him.

"Well, if it's that important I suppose so. You'll have to take your shoes off you know and they'll probably insist you hire a long skirt or apron. They don't like people going in in shorts."

"Oh, thank you sir. I understand sir." And with that he rushed up the steps.

"Oh, there you are!" I turned to meet my second flushed and dishevelled person.

This time it was Roy. A little way behind him were most of the rest of the boys, hurrying along with a small pack of local youths snapping at their heels.

"Have you seen David Tite, headmaster?"

"Yes. He's just gone on ahead into the mosque. Why…" "Thank God for that." His relief was palpable.

"Roy, would you please tell me what is going on…but first can't you put a stop to that stupid fracas. What on earth has got into them? And who are the boys you've brought?"

It was probably the two approaching policemen rather than Roy's resolute bellowing which persuaded the home side to back off. I used the respite to hustle Roy and the boys into the mosque.

"Now Roy," I said as we were slipping off our shoes by the entrance. "Before we step another yard, tell me what's been happening."

"It's all the fault of that fool Tite…"

As is the case in many cities, street trading in Istanbul is unofficially organised into 'territories' by self-appointed leaders of competing and jealous syndicates. An eight-year-old shoeshine boy needs protection to prevent fifteen-year-old bullies muscling in on his patch and the price is a cut to the syndicate from his already meagre takings. And so, it goes on up the 'food chain'. Perhaps then, some good comes from the system but enforcement is inevitably closely allied to intimidation and violence and disputes can end very nastily. As an outsider to the 'system', no matter how jocular and temporary the intent, once he had set himself up as a trader, David was inviting trouble and, according to the rest of the boys, it wasn't long in coming. Intoxicated by early sales successes and dazzled by conceit at his own cleverness, David's reaction to protest and remonstrance from the street establishment had been cheap and cheerful defiance. The presence about him of his friends, themselves sadly finding easy amusement in his folly, only served to encourage him. The end, when it came, apparently took all our lot by surprise, that in itself being an indictment of their naivety. In a flash David's unsold flutes had been seized and smashed and, after a couple of half- hearted kicks and punches, a scrappy chase, marked by barracking rather than assault, had followed.

Excited and unsettled as they were by these events, it took a little time and effort before I got the boys' thoughts properly on the cerulean glories of the mosque's awe-inspiring interior. We were more than half-way round our tour of the mosque when it struck me that David hadn't re-joined us. Where on earth was the silly boy now? A few moments later we came across a class of young Turkish boys sitting on the floor, hanging on to every word the young cleric in charge of them was saying. It was a touching and moving sight and put me in mind of the annual Confirmation classes held in our own school. At that precise

59

moment I spotted David. There he was, *in the class,* sitting tailor-fashion in the back row, sharing a copy of the Koran with another boy.

The pose and posture were perfect. Sad to say this was no conversion driven by acquired grace but a cunning camouflage should his foes have followed him into this blue-tiled world of light and shadow. A silly boy if ever there was one, I thought. But then I thought again. A born survivor, I concluded.

One of the stranger features of the Ottoman Empire was the *devshirme* —the annual tax levied on Christian families— which took the form of a compulsory 'harvest' of boys at the age of about fourteen for a lifetime of military service in the *Janissaries,* the Sultan's elite army corps. One such Christian youth, taken from his family and made to serve in several of Sultan Suleyman, the Magnificent's campaigns, was Mimar Sinan, born about 1497, At some stage he was transferred to the Sultan's personal service and became his Chief Architect around 1450. Suleyman was the greatest of the Ottoman sultans, expanding the bounds of the Ottoman Empire to the very gates of Vienna and Sinan was the finest architect the Levant ever produced. The two men together created the incomparable *Suleymaniye,* the majestic mosque complex which is widely regarded as Istanbul's most glorious Ottoman era structure. Sinan, by the way, worked well into his nineties and is said to be responsible for almost five hundred buildings scattered over both the European and Asian dominions of the Ottoman Empire. We busily devoted a long afternoon to visiting, first the Suleymaniye and then the Topkapi Sarayi', the great palace and harem of the Sultans.

Reflecting on the morning's troubles, I found myself contemplating the possible merits of a modern-day cull of certain Christian youths for compulsory military service but my malevolent thoughts instantly evaporated under the Suleymaniye's sublime spell.

Completed in 1557, its vast and overwhelming interior reflected its status as the most important of all the imperial mosques. The interior furnishings and decoration of this sumptuous mosque are of great distinction, the wooden surfaces of the door, window shutters and bookcases, for example, being superbly carved and encrusted with ivory and mother-of-pearl. It must be emphasised that this mosque, enormous as it is, occupies only a fraction of the *kulliye* or overall mosque complex. Other elements that were part of the Suleymaniye included several *madrassas* (religious schools), a medical college and hospital, Turkish baths, the *'imaret'* (the place where mosque employees and thousands of poor people were fed each day) and the caravanserai. Among the associated gardens are several tombs incorporating tilework of exquisite quality, including the resting place of Roxelana, Suleyman's favourite wife.

For close on four hundred years the Topkapi Palace was the theatre in which the rise and fall of the Ottoman Empire was written and acted out. Be it bureaucratic routine or court ritual, be it bizarre drama or labyrinthine political intrigue, History has seldom come up with anything as extraordinary as the world within the Topkapi and by comparison, Louis *XIV's* Versailles was a mere Sunday school. It was from the Topkapi's hidden closets that powerful armies were directed and sent out to conquer territories in Europe and Asia; it was from its jewelled courts that great, as well as deplorable, sultans ruled. It was in salons sheathed in wondrous Iznik tiles where unlucky sultans were treacherously assassinated or more resolute ones themselves butchered their royal siblings.

At one time more than five thousand people lived within: slaves and eunuchs, concubines and viziers, ministers and Janissaries of the Guard. All their needs and functions were reflected in the kaleidoscope of separate buildings, courts and pavilions and in the warren of terraces, screens and passageways that made up this extraordinary palace. The very titles borne by each secluded sanctum intoxicate the imagination. The Terrace of the Favourites, The Circumcision Room, the Court of the Divan, the Gilded Cage, the Office of the Grand Vizier, the Hall of the Black Eunuchs, the Gate of the Watchman of the Girls and the Residence of the Chief Executioner – the latter having its own fountain where the office holder could wash his hands after duty. And these are but a sample.

Nowadays, in the Topkapi's role as a national museum, numerous rooms display Ottoman arts and artefacts. These range from paintings through to the clothes and jewels worn by the Sultans and from period kitchen utensils to an incomparable collection of Chinese porcelain.

Schoolboys, as I've mentioned already, tend to lack staying power when it comes to touring museums and monuments but the Topkap'i Saray'i held our lot enthralled from start to finish. But then, what fifteen-year-old would have no interest in touring a harem or in looking upon the couch where Sultan Marat III sired his one hundred and three children?

I had solemnly promised that we would devote our third day in Istanbul to the delights of the Kapali Carsi, the Covered Bazaar of sixty-one streets and four thousand shops. However, braving murmurs of youthful discontent, I insisted, as a curtain raiser to their shopaholic ambitions, on a brief early morning excursion to a final clutch of Stamboulian gems. First, I had unwashed faces and sleepy eyes study a stretch of the ten-mile city walls, which go in a great arc from the Sea of Marmara to the Golden Horn. The neighbourhood just inside the part of the wall we selected is one of the most picturesque in Istanbul, with country lanes meandering through the gardens lying in their shadow. There we found a restaurant and ordered a regal breakfast of omelettes, honeyed cakes and coffee from its astonished proprietor whom we had ambushed as he was taking down his shutters. The troops were now in a better temper as I carted them off to view the Emperor Valens' imposing aqueduct, built in AD 375. Next it was on to Justinian's huge underground cistern, a boundless half-drowned forest of vaulted columns receding into an echoey, Stygian distance. Finally, we took a criminally short look at the church of Saint Saviour in Chora, site of Istanbul's best mosaics – and emerged into a drenching thunderstorm.

No one ever forgets his first visit to Istanbul's great covered bazaar. It is a wonderland that would make Alice green with envy and El Dorado look like a corner shop. You can buy a plan of sorts near the entrances but don't bother. It is far more fun to take this retail Niagara in a barrel and plunge straight in. The first waves are almost overwhelming. The pungent odour of vanilla beans and the racy smell of cloves batter the nostrils. But *courage mes enfants* for not until we reach the street of the aphrodisiac stalls will you know what the word *aroma* really means! The ears, too, are assaulted by the cacophony of a thousand effusive salesmen to which you must add the noisy labours of hammering craftsmen, for many shops are workshops too. And the eyes? Do you for a moment suppose they are not bedazzled and hypnotised when instantly confronted by a hundred singular sights? See that *hamal* or market porter bent double under his enormous load and see, too, that up-from-the-country peasant farmer with his black-shrouded wife walking three respectful feet to his rear. And don't miss the itinerant coffee vendor. He's the creature *within* that shining black contraption that resembles Stephenson's Rocket. You ask what the small boy wants who is tugging at your sleeve? At a guess he's been sent out to fetch customers for his master's carpet shop. All right, if you wish, let us follow him.

"What sort of carpet, sir, do you have in mind?" a lean hawk-faced man courteously enquires as he provides you with a chair and sends the boy off to get you coffee or apple tea. "New or possibly a certified antique? A silk one from Hereke? Or perhaps a wool and cotton *taban,* handmade in Kanya? Not carrying much cash? That's no problem, sir. My boy will deliver to your hotel. Too expensive? Of course I understand. What price would you like to pay?"

Ah, naming a low price will not save you for, nothing daunted, the fellow deftly unrolls carpet number twenty-three at exactly the price you named. You will have to show real character to escape this fellow's clutches!

The range of stall and shop is practically endless and there are literally thousands of venues, yet, as you wander around you begin to sense the order of things in this city within a city. This street is clothing, that is luggage. Here we have a silversmith and there, half a dozen shops selling exquisite glassware. A jewelled sword? A broom? A humble plastic bowl? All can be found.

A fascinating ploy with some specialist items is to trace the goods backwards from outlet to source. We are soon in a maze of alleyways which lead beyond the bazaar into cobbled streets rich in animal and industrial odours. Beyond a pair of rusty tin-sheeted gates and up a set of rickety stairs, we reach a flimsy landing. In through a door, we try desperately to adjust our eyes to the gloom. The room is tiny and oven-hot, but our young guide gently nudges and pushes until six or seven of us are within. Besides our own, the room is already full of boys. Six of them. But are they ten-year-olds? Twelve? Or stunted fifteens? Who knows? They all look remarkably alike and never pause from their hammering and cutting and polishing. Bright, nicely tooled copper jugs and plates are stacked around. A punching machine clatters away in a corner while nimble little fingers feed it bits of copper and somehow avoid its oscillating fangs. Two lads wearing tinted specs solder on handles. We nod our thanks and emerge into light and fresh air and guilty silence.

"My God," exclaimed Adrian at length.

"Do they work there like that every day?" asked Tom, turning to me. "What about school?"

"You've just seen another world, my friends. It *is* like that every day and I shouldn't think there will any school."

My young companions remained silent and thoughtful all the way back to the Kapali Carsi. And so did I. In truth there was little to be said and much to think on.

Chapter 8

Early on the first day of August we crossed into Asia, doing so two hundred feet above the Bosporus on the great new bridge built in 1973 to mark the fiftieth anniversary of the founding of the Turkish Republic. At the time it was the fourth largest suspension bridge in the world and had been built by Dorman Long Ltd of Middlesbrough, hometown to several in our party.

The Asian part of Turkey, often referred to as Anatolia, is huge, being almost one and a half times the area of France. Its east-to-west extent is nearly a thousand miles (London to Edinburgh is a mere four hundred) and is about five hundred from north to south. The great bulk of Anatolia is taken up by a high arid plateau whose eastern half has an average height of more than 6,500 feet. And its climate is much the same as the Russian steppes: in January the thermometer can fall to minus 40°C whereas, in contrast, in July it often rises to a searing forty above. Access to this plateau is barred by daunting mountain ramparts. In the north, separating the plateau from the Black Sea coastal fringe, are the Pontin mountains whose highest peaks soar to within a whisker of 13,000 feet. Guarding the Mediterranean south is the even mightier Taurus range.

If this almost boundless hinterland imposed disheartening daily mileages on our schedule, it also opened up the prospect of a real wilderness experience. Here, on the banks of remote rivers and little-known lakes we would be able to camp as Nature intended. We would roast our meat on a real fire, wash our travel-stained bodies in clear, gravel-bottomed streams and fall asleep under the stars.

Anatolia has played host to a long series of succeeding races, empires, creeds and civilisations. Hittites and Celts, Persians and Greeks, Romans and Byzantines, Christians and Muslims. The Turks are only the latest layer, and it is easy to forget that this ninety-eight percent Muslim country was once both the cradle and the powerhouse of Christianity. Cappadocia was visited by Saint Paul and its Christian people were directly addressed in Saint Peter's first epistle.

Travelling via Ankara, we arrived on Thursday August Second. Travellers often describe the area around UrgUp and Goreme as Geology's great joke. Volcanic eruptions long ago smothered much of Cappadocia under a thick

64

covering of ash and mud which further geological activity compressed into a soft rock known as *tufa.* Deposited at the same time and lying randomly within the *tufa,* are clumps of hard basalt. The weathering of this mix of hard and soft rock over following aeons has created fantastic canyons and gorges and has sculptured from the banded rocks incredible crags, turrets and cones in a colourful wonderland of geological 'liquorice all sorts'. Many of the cones, which are the most common shape, stand over a hundred feet tall, some alone and others clustered like cohorts of giants. Those which are capped by huge lumps of precariously balanced basalt are known to the locals as 'fairy chimneys'. And, as if these playthings of Nature were not already freakish to excess, Man has added his own touch by cutting and carving and by excavating and tunnelling, to create houses, refuges, churches and whole townships out of the living rock. There are said to be over a hundred rupestrian churches in the Goreme area alone, many of them elaborately sculptured and adorned with riotous frescos, capturing for succeeding generations the religious visions of Byzantine Christianity. It was eerie and yet thrilling, to wander round these stone-cool, hollowed-out homes and churches. It was also quite hazardous as in places further natural erosion had resulted in some passageways abruptly ending as a stark hole high up a cliff face. At one place we saw where a complete church has been vertically sliced, half having fallen away to leave a complete elevation in section. The occupation of these Christian rock dwellings did not wholly end with the capture of Anatolia by Islamic Turks and the tolerated remnants of their Greek populations eked out an existence in a handful of rupestrian settlements until the first quarter of the twentieth century.

It was in the lunar landscape of Cappadocia that our party suffered its first medical emergency. Predictably enough, the phantasmagorical appearance of the rock formations immediately attracted the sturdy limbs of vigorous boyhood, eroded nooks and crannies promising excellent holds by which to clamber up their gritty heights. For the most part the exploration, if rather noisy, was judicious; delighted shouts constantly advertising a discovered cave or especially curious formation. But a little knowledge can be a dangerous thing and Philip Cairns, just turned fifteen and an enthusiastic member of the school's rock-climbing club, had greater ambitions. A pair of haycock-shaped cones, perhaps thirty feet high with scarcely a foot between them at their bases, offered the prospect of triumphant conquest if correct chimneying techniques could be applied to overcome the near-vertical lower section. A tall, blond lad this Phil

Cairns; long limbed and athletic. Open natured tooand refreshingly truthful but quite a creator of untoward classroom events where a teacher's hand was inexperienced or unwisely light. And there he was when I first spotted what he was up to, his fair hair haloed by the sun as he waved a Union Jack and postured on the exposed summit in mimicry of a Hillary or a Tenzing.

Grief came during the descent. One second his feet had a friction purchase on the gritty rock and the next they didn.t. It was a long agonising slide down Nature's vicious sandpaper and it was made worse by short sleeves and shorts. Youthful subtleness and the rasping friction of the rock saved broken bones; but at the cost of a lot of skin and we all looked in horror at the wide extent of his raw and bleeding flesh. We were pretty well equipped as far as First Aid was concerned but First Aid supplies are Spartan things. Sterile dressings and stinging germicides addressed the medical imperatives, but we could do nothing about the searing agony. With his peers looking on half-fascinated and half-flinchingly, Phil had little choice but to play the man. He impressed us all.

"Sir, the driver of the truck wants to know if we have a gun."

I had been busy refuelling the bus just outside the ancient city of Kayseri (the Caesarea of the New Testament) when Alan Beattie, one of our tall, sinewy sixteen-year-olds whose sharply chiselled features reflected his forceful nature, had delivered his arresting message. My surprise clearly matched his hopes for his face cracked into a broad grin and his eyes danced with mischief. He had, nonetheless spoken the truth. A small gipsy-looking fellow, perched on the mudguard of his enormous truck attending to its engine, jumped lightly down to the ground as I approached, and it was plain he was keen to have a word.

"You go to Sivas?" he asked bluntly. "Many bad places. You haff gun?"

A Hungarian, bound for Budapest with a load of edible nuts, he spoke earnestly about bandits operating in the high mountain passes over which we would travel before descending to meet the main eastern highway at Sivas. He hadn't the English to explain in detail but judging from his affectionate caressing of a squat automatic he'd suddenly pulled from his trouser pocket, it seemed clear enough from his mimed actions that he was claiming the necessity of recent usage in self-defence. Although our own weaponry was limited to a single heavy machete, my scepticism far outweighed my concern. Roy was of the same mind.

"It was hardly likely," Roy had asserted as we resumed our journey "that the Turkish government would tolerate such lawlessness. Hang it all," he went on, "everyone knows how tough their police can be."

About three hours later we had pulled off the steep, winding road to stretch our legs and organise a bite to eat. The distant view down to a river, perhaps two thousand feet below our vantage point, superb as it was, was rivalled close at hand by an extraordinary profusion of wildflowers that carpeted every last inch of soil. Rocky outcrops and a liberal scattering of boulders great and small populated the entire landscape. But there wasn't a tree in sight and, we and the flowers excepted, it seemed there wasn't another living thing for miles around.

Wrong! Half-listening to a couple of boys squabbling about whose turn it was to do some chore, my drifting eyes alighted on a cairn some eighty or so yards away and I was startled to see a boy sitting on the top of it. Startled a little because he wasn't one of ours but startled a lot because he was holding a rifle and was clearly stationed on guard. I had scarcely taken in the intelligence of it when other figures began to emerge from shadowy spaces among some house-sized rocks dead ahead. It seemed amazing that they should have come so close before I had noticed them, and it brought home to me how these rock-strewn landscapes could rival a forest in providing refuges and hiding places.

At first it was sheep and cattle that came into view, perhaps fifty or sixty of them, but soon after men on horses, flanked by large dogs, appeared. Most of the men were bearded and all were swarthy. The column of animals trudged rhythmically past us, holding their course and staring ahead with lacklustre eyes, but when the men came alongside, they halted and looked us carefully over. All, I noted, had rifles slung across their shoulders.

There was no language between us, but we hailed them and they gave us cautious nods. Their boy came off his lookout and met a couple of ours as he made to join his masters. In silence the two employed the mysterious bond of youth to ask the why and wherefore of bearing arms and in silent pride the one made his reasons known. A bridge thus built, chunks of homemade English fruit cake were shared around, admiration of the great dogs expressed and the shepherd boy, for a keepsake, given the dented aluminium water canteen he clearly fancied. And from this meagre intercourse we learned that the dogs were kept, in the main, to keep four-legged winter wolves at bay. The rifles, it seemed, were also borne because of other 'wolves': These an all-season species of two-legged ones. In silent reflection I apologised to the Hungarian truck driver.

Sheep throwing is not some cruel Turkish sport which will have to be banned before Turkey can be considered for membership of the European Union. It would appear to be in some areas, however, the only practicable way of

67

transferring sheep from one pasture to another. We came across the practice deep in eastern

Anatolia whilst our road was hair-pinning its way from the high barren plateau towards a lush green valley peppered with eucalyptus trees.

"Look at those guys down there chucking sheep into the river."

The shrill voice of our informant achieved immediate impact within the bus. Rubric cubes stopped mid twist, abruptly neglected chess sets slipped off sunburnt knees and lurid paperbacks were slammed shut as their readers craned their necks to follow Tom's excited pointing. Even Slackie, prone and half-asleep at his favourite spot on the floor between the rows of seats, levered himself up to take a look. While half an hour at most sees a school minibus traverse the entire heathery brown expanses of the North York moors, crossing the grassy brown uplands of Anatolia has to be computed in whole days of virtually unchanging landscapes. Accordingly, my young fellow- adventurers may surely be forgiven their indifference to the passing scenery where a glimpsed shepherd boy and flock may well be the sole event in half a morning's travel.

As we descended towards the valley floor, we could see those hundreds of fat-tailed sheep had been densely penned by the river's edge and were kept there by posted men and dogs, whilst the river itself was a scene of puzzling confusion. Certainly, it all looked interesting enough to be worth a stop and after a further two or three descending zigs and zags we were able to leave the highway and crawl in low gear down a track running right down to the river.

About thirty yards wide with rocky shallows on our side, on the far bank the river was deep and fast-flowing. Half a dozen hunky men in flat caps and checked shirts were busy, as Tom had rightly said, seizing sheep one by one before pitching them into the river. Standing side-on to the bank, each sheep-thrower would thrust his hands deep into the long wool of the sheep's back, jerk the animal up into the air and then, in a single move of rhythm and power, swing himself round to pitch it as far across the river as he could. The action was continuous and flowing, almost like a dance and the air was thick with flying sheep and the spouts of water thrown up by their noisy splash- downs.

Standing waist-deep in the water like rows of steppingstones were a dozen boys whose task it was to catch hold of each landing sheep and manoeuvre it like a passed parcel from boy to boy until it reached the far shallows. There, setting it on its feet and giving its backside a rough clout, the last boy encouraged the bemused beast to head for the shore and join its comrades in pastures new. For the most part the throwers achieved the target zone with remarkable consistency but every now and then a rebellious sheep would resist and in the resulting struggle cause the thrower to muff his aim. Almost always this meant the creature fell short, ending up in the fast, deep water to be swept away in the racing current. Such an event was the occasion for much shouting and whistling and a couple of the biggest boys would then take off in pursuit, swimming after the errant beast until it could be collared and pulled into shallow water. None were lost but a few were taken for a hundred yards or more, the heaving chests and watery coughs and splutters of the returning rescuers bearing witness to the heavy labour entailed.

"I wish I was in there helping," exclaimed a wistful David Armstrong, himself a farmer's son. "It looks more like fun than work to me."

"Sir," called another, "is there time for a swim? It's been as hot as hell in the bus."

I'm always wary of mixing boys and rivers, there being too many unknowns in the safety equation for my liking, but David was built like an ox and was a fine swimmer. Had we here, I suddenly wondered, an opportunity to give some of the gang a little adventure to remember alongside their recollections of the sheep throwing?

"Do you think you could manage? The rescue stuff I mean."

"I don't see why not."

"Would you really like to have a go at helping?"

He looked hard at me; incredulity, hope and then delight successively flashing across his face. "Can I really?"

"I don't see why not," I echoed, suddenly coming to a decision. "They all need a wash, that's for sure," added Roy.

"Ah, I wasn't thinking of everyone. Just Dave here and, well, perhaps a couple of the other oldest ones if they want."

Discrimination between boys in a single group is always difficult but the deep part of the river needed respect. Chasing after swept away sheep involved a mix of running through the stony shallows and powerful swimming and even the Turks were leaving this work to their oldest boys. David, Craig Bradley and Adrian Meynell stripped off by the bus and then gleefully hurried down to the river.

The Turks, as ever spontaneously positive and welcoming, hailed the intervention, though I suspected the amused glances they gave one another owed much to the prospect of laughs at our expense. David Armstrong and Company, however, did us proud, retrieving two sheep on their own and assisting a struggling Turkish boy over a third, which was a large and uncooperative ram.

We didn't stay helping and watching all that long. Besides having our journey schedule to think about, the water was much colder than any had bargained for and our three stalwarts had emerged with chattering teeth as well as sundry cuts and bruises. How the younger Turkish boys managed to stick at it in such cold water I don't know, for it must have taken them all of two hours to get their whole flock across the water.

Erzurum is the largest and most important city in eastern Anatolia. It is a sombre and rather colourless place, isolated on the harsh and barren high plateau with the rough and ready appearance of a frontier garrison town – a role often conferred upon it during its long and eventful history. It must be a miserable place in winter, being six and a half thousand feet above sea level and ringed by mountains almost touching the ten thousand mark. Erzurum contains a handful of ancient buildings, the most notable being the Hatuniye Medrese. This one-time theological college (it is now a museum) takes its name from its pair of tall, parallel and fluted minarets and when viewed end-on, the elevation resembles a miniature version of Battersea power station.

The population density of eastern Anatolia is much lower than in the rest of Turkey and this is very noticeable as the Iranian frontier is approached. Towns and villages become fewer and farther between and they are poorer and more primitive. The great plateau seems wilder and less touched by man and the mountains grander and more awesome. And no mountain in Turkey is grander or more awesome than Mount Ararat (Agri Dagi), the mountain which tradition asserts was where Noah's Ark first grounded at the end of the Flood. Logically therefore, it is considered by biblical literalists as the centre from which Mankind once again spread throughout the world.

Forming part of the mountain wall separating eastern Anatolia from the mighty Caucasians in nearby Russia and Armenia, Mount Ararat stands at 16,854 feet (5137 m) high and, so starkly does it rise above the surrounding plain, that it is visible almost a hundred miles away. It was Saturday 4th of August when we drove along the great eastern highway from Erzurum towards the steppes and deserts of middle Asia and it was here, on the old Silk Road, where we first had to share our road with stately lines of loaded camels.

70

Just after midday on that same road the snowy cone of Ararat was first spotted in the far distance and three hours later its bulk was totally dominating the northern horizon. We made camp in a sheltered hollow some three or four miles away from the main highway, stopping long before nightfall to give ourselves time to mark our last night in Turkey with a special dinner. I had even bought a couple of bottles of wine – of dubious provenance – in Erzurum for the purpose. Tomorrow would bring Iran and its fearsome ayatollahs but for this special night we would have a merry campfire to succour our jaded bodies and enjoy a stunning view of Ararat's glistening slopes, made glorious pink in the red sunset, to feast our souls.

Chapter 9

At the Iranian frontier post at Bazargan the heat was far beyond anything we had previously experienced and it was made worse by an oven-hot wind which blew stinging dust devils all around the buildings and vehicles. A couple of taxis, two or three trucks and about half a dozen long-distance buses were already at the post when we arrived, each bus having a mob of waiting passengers. Many, in their enveloping black *chadors,* were squatting among their luggage waiting for customs staff to check them through. For the most part their luggage was in the form of large roped-up cartons or great onion-shaped cloth bundles and both sorts must have given the customs men a hard time. A soldier, poor devil, his machine-gun carelessly dumped on the top of his sun-baked sandbagged enclosure, frizzled and yawned.

I had already made sure the boys were wearing long trousers and long-sleeved shirts, as required by the Islamic dress code of Iran's new masters. With the country at war, who knew what powers these frontier officials might wield? for all the hard-won visas which I was firmly clasping in my hands, I couldn't throw off the feeling that our entrance into the territory of such a touchy and suspicious regime was far from guaranteed and so at all costs we would have to show cheerful cooperation whatever red tape and petty irritations they might throw our way. We were plainly the only Europeans around and the moment we entered the 'Passport Control' building I felt we were as obviously alien as nuns in a betting shop.

Several identical poster portraits of the Ayatollah Khomeini glowered down at us from the stained and flaking walls and their eyes seemed to follow us in the queue as we inched slowly forward. For a few moments we won some slight relief from the suffocating heat as our section of the queue moved beneath the one and only working fan of the eight hanging down from the fly-blown ceiling. But it was a mixed blessing. The long stalk attaching the fan to the ceiling wobbled alarmingly and seemed likely to work itself loose at any moment and so I was glad when we had shuffled out of its scything range.

About twenty yards from the actual passport counter the queue was filing alongside somenoticeboards, all displaying pages from newspapers. Everything, of course, was in Persian script and took the form of column after column of words, broken here and there by small passport sized photographs. For one thoughtless moment I imagined it all had something to do with people 'wanted' for passport offences but then the awful truth dawned and I felt a sudden guilt. That these displayed columns were a listing of battle casualties in the madcap conflict being waged in the south against Iraq was now horribly obvious and my initial ignorance made me feel as if I had insulted to the fallen. The merest glance made it equally apparent that thousands were listed here and that many who had died, as the photographs made plain, had scarcely been old enough to have passed from boy to man. In a hoarse whisper, which somehow seemed to suit the moment, I explained to the boys the significance of the displayed newsprint, pointing out that in 1916 the London papers had probably carried similar lists during the slaughter on the Somme.

Just as I finished and one or two of them had started asking me questions, a tall elderly Iranian left his place in the queue and came up to me. He spoke in a soft, dignified voice, presumably in Iranian and of course I understood not a word. The eyes which held mine were moist and I sensed that the saying of the words was what mattered to him rather than my understanding them. There was a murmur of approval from the queue as a whole as he finished. He then shuffled over to where our boys were standing and embraced a couple of them, looking closely into their faces and squeezing their shoulders, all the while sadly shaking his head. As the old man returned to his place, in some unaccountable and intangible way, the ambience in the building had been transformed. I felt suddenly a good deal more comfortable.

"Welcome to Iran," said the official at the counter as I dumped all our passports and visas in front of him.

As I have already indicated, it had been obvious from the earliest stages in the planning of our overland journey to India that the volatile situation in revolutionary Iran would be a storm cloud constantly hovering over us and an ever-present threat to the realisation of our aim. Once we had begun our journey, we were to a degree out of touch with world news and all the while we were making our way through Europe and Turkey, I kept wondering how the Iran-Iraq war was faring and what news there might be from Tehran. In Istanbul I had telephoned the school to learn what had been said in the latest Telex from the

ICI office in Tehran to the school governors – an arrangement kindly offered by ICI's Billingham HQ given so many of our pupils came from families with ICI connections. The Telex, given its source, was authoritative but nonetheless wasn't exactly brimming with useful detail. It had simply read: 'No significant political developments in Tehran'.

Now, in the actual moment of entering Iran and seeing the place thick with banners and posters proclaiming the anger of Islam and the promise of divine vengeance against Britain, the United States and Israel; I was finding it hard to shake off an increasing sense of doubt and even of crass misjudgement. What was I doing, I kept asking myself, taking a busload of teenagers into a war-torn land ruled by a bunch of murderous religious cranks? Didn't I realise that only a couple of years back, fanatical supporters of this same regime had seized a hundred or so American hostages and all but brought down the Carter presidency in the process? Wasn't the truth of the matter that I had allowed the success of a few previous school expeditions to go to my head and had now bitten off far more than I could chew? It might have been all very well back in England to rabbit on about the war being two or three hundred miles away from the route we would use but weren't battle lines, particularly in modern warfare, apt to shift with dramatic speed and scant warning?

Reminding myself that a good deal of thought had been given early on to strategies we might employ if our reception in Iran turned out to be at all unfriendly, far from bringing reassurance, now seemed to be telling me that possession of a 'contingency plan' at all was more like evidence of folly than of sensible provision for a possible difficulty. Surely the *responsible* answer to the possibility of encountering danger during our transit through Iran should have been to rule out travelling there in the first place – the consequential abandonment of the India project being a small price to pay where the safety of pupils was concerned. And yet? Thanks to the old man's speech and its effect on the Iranians around and about us, I was now on the way to feeling relaxed again. Optimistic even. "Welcome to Iran" the man at the Passport Control counter had said. Who knows? Perhaps we would be!

Our basic plan was to travel along the main highway from the Turkish frontier as far as important city of Tabriz whereupon we would turn north-east to the shores of the Caspian Sea. Once there, the idea was to skirt round the Caspian's southern shore to the city of Sari and then continue due east to Mashhad. After that we would turn south and brave the thousand-kilometre

74

rough road across the Great Persian Desert (the Dasht-e-Lut) to Zahedan, which lay close to the Pakistan border. There were several considerations behind this choice of route. First, it would enable us at all times to keep ourselves at the farthest possible distance from the war zone. Second, we would avoid Tehran. Tehran was the heart and powerhouse of the Iranian Islamic Revolution and it was there that most of the religious fanaticism lay. It was therefore the place most likely to throw up people hostile to Westerners. Additionally, it was widely acknowledged that cutting out Tehran would be no great sacrifice with respect to seeing the sights; most guidebooks putting pollution, chronic overcrowding, and a dearth of any sights worth seeing as Tehran's most notable attributes.

"Aesthetically a complete mess," said one well known guide and another similar one commented that "even the most mendacious travel agent would be hard put to find a sight to praise in this sprawling and largely squalid capital." In contrast, according to the same guidebook, the Caspian coast would be green and pleasant and the people living there 'the friendliest of all Iranians'. As it happened, we were not able to test these assertions for in the end we never went to the Caspian at all.

Tabriz, a very large and ancient city and the first major Iranian urban centre we encountered proved to be both interesting and, to my huge relief, friendly. Thanks to the fierceness of the Iran-Iraq war and the excesses of revolutionary fervour widely reported in the West, in the years following the fall of the Shah foreign visitors were a rare species in Iran, this being especially the case in provincial cities away from Tehran. In consequence, the arrival of our modest right-hand drive bus, packed with pink-skinned European youngsters became an immediate sensation wherever we went.

You need to bear in mind that most towns and cities of the Middle East are thick with unemployed or under-employed young males who have little choice but to hang around their town squares and like focal points, craving of course for some event or opportunity that might just chance to make their current hour distinct from the previous empty thousand and this fact of course tended to amplify the star-burst effect of our appearance.

Given the natural openness of youth, all these encounters were marked by friendly and positive enquiry as to the why and wherefore of our presence in their country. The thirst of young Iranians for any scrap of information about 'life in the West' or concerning our views of their country and its situation was unquenchable. So encouraged, our travel proceeded in an atmosphere of increasing confidence and we even began to enquire openly about our likely reception in Tehran and heard nothing at all worrying. Indeed, in contrast when we discussed our proposed crossing of the Great Persian Desert between Mashhad and Zahedan with manager of a petrol station who happened to speak pretty good English, he became quite emotional as he set out to dissuade us from any such idea.

"That road go very near to Afghanistan," he said, pulling a face and shaking his head. "Benzene (i.e.fuel) not there many times. Big problems for you. And road very bad with much sand." He finished up by warning us about Afghan bandits and how the road virtually petered out in places making it easy to get lost in the waterless wastes. And just in case we still hadn't got the message, he grabbed one of his garage lads by the hair and, with marked violence, mimed the cutting of his throat.

"Many Afghans!" He finished, shaking his head and spitting with inelegant vigour.

Chapter 10

The open friendliness of the people we met in Tabriz and the other towns we passed through and their spontaneous interest in our journey triggered in me more than mere relief. Steadily creeping into my mind was a feeling that I had been too pessimistic about Iran and had taken on board all the facile assumptions of an ever- excitable Western Press. The notion of slipping through this immense and fascinating land, essentially unnoticed and disengaged, was beginning to seem like a wasted opportunity. By taking to quiet byways and shyly avoiding Persia's great historic cities, would I not rob my splendid young companions of a truly fantastic experience? What other British schoolboys – or citizens for that matter – had visas giving them official permission to transit the very heartland of Revolutionary Iran? These thoughts and of course their less buoyant and deeply sobering 'but what if?' Opposites, coursed through my mind as we covered the long miles of this leg of our journey to India.

When we reached Qazvin, the place where the road to the Caspian splits off from the Tehran-bound highway we were on, we halted for a bite to eat. Leaving Roy and his merry meal-duties boys to sort out the domestics, I stole a few moments to run the issues of the moment through my mind. It was clearly decision time.

Bearing in mind the compelling advice of the petrol station manager, using the roundabout route via the Caspian shore was not going to be as straightforward as I had originally supposed and, *if* our reception so far was anything to go by, passing through Tehran was beginning to look perfectly viable and, indeed, sensible. But…however much I mulled the matter over, I remained dogged by the same old nagging uncertainties.

As much to clear my own thoughts as anything, I decided to involve the entire party in the debate. The boys at first were, I think, a little taken aback at being consulted – in a school ambience is not the Head supposed to have all the answers? – But soon began making well-reasoned comments and when the decision to go by the direct route through Tehran was made, I felt confident that at least everyone was aware of how things stood and what was involved,

Nonetheless, as the miles rolled by and we stoically endured the heat and dust of summer travel across Iran's desiccated and mountainous northern provinces, my inner thoughts were increasingly monopolised by the question of how things might be in Tehran, this being particularly so as its sprawling and ugly outer suburbs began to crowd in upon the highway. At one place, where a collision between a pair of large trucks had forced all the traffic to a standstill, out of the blue a crowd of young men shouting and waving their arms suddenly surrounded our bus. My instinctive reaction was to wind up my window quickly and, according to Roy, look very scared! I'll not deny it! And I must have looked a mighty lot more scared seconds later when they actually wrenched open the opposite door! However, the invaders, for all their boisterous and uncouth behaviour were all smiles.

'Hullo mister' and 'you America?' Would be a fair sample of their strident greetings. Handshakes and pats on shoulders followed until police whistles blew and we were thus obliged to move on – shaken and yet somehow slightly cheered.

We knew we had truly entered the lions' den when we came to the Azadi monument. This huge stone tower, shaped like an inverted letter 'Y', stands at the centre of an enormous traffic circus at the northern approach to the capital. Originally commissioned by the Shah in 1971 to commemorate Persia's two and a half thousand years of empire, after his overthrow it became, with fitting irony, the iconic symbol of the new Shia Islamic revolutionary regime. At the same time its name, in deference to the needs of political agendas, was changed from the Shahyad Tower to the Azadi (Peace) Tower.

All along this phase of our journey, the nearer we got to Tehran the more flags, banners and posters supporting the Ayatollah Khomeini and his rule over all aspects of Iranian life there were to be seen. Here at the Azadi Tower, however, the fantastic riot of banners, posters and shouting supporters was like an overwhelming blizzard.

Within this bewildering maelstrom of politically driven frenzy, the greatest worry of all, as I steered our precious bus cautiously among the manic traffic, were the minibuses and pick-up trucks filled to overflowing with noisy and heavily armed young supporters of the Revolution, many of them members of the much-feared Revolutionary Guards. Their precise aim was not easy to fathom for they appeared to be simply driving round and round the traffic circus as fast and as intimidatingly as possible, waving weapons and shouting slogans.

If it had been the actual day of the Shah's overthrow, we might have expected such hysterical goings on; even perhaps if it had been simply the anniversary date of the event. But now in August 1984 those seismic upheavals were some five and a half years in the past, so what explanation is there for the riotous hubbub we experienced? Putting the question later on to Iranians we met it seems that whenever an event occurred – in or out of Iran – which could be said to manifest some set-back or disadvantage to the Ayatollah's regime, his turbulent and most fanatical supporters would respond by taking to the streets and put on these terrifying displays of solidarity.

Even setting aside the extreme motoring frolics of the Revolutionary Guards and their like, the antics of the ordinary Tehran motorist going about his mundane domestic business were apt to shred even the most sanguine nerves. Next to no-one appeared to obey traffic lights and each and every intersection was marked by an anarchy of blasting horns, revving engines and shouted driver-to-driver abuse. I once counted six youths clinging on to the one motorbike: Four to one machine was commonplace. Set within this tempestuous sea of relatively small fry, majestic Leyland double-deckers ploughed along with their oven-baked passengers hanging out of the glassless barred windows. Dozens more passengers travelled externally wherever some foot or handhold could be seized. Given the cheapness of fuel in this oil-rich land, nobody appeared to care one jot about engine efficiency and just about every other vehicle spewed forth a trail of filthy smoke. The city in fact was more or less permanently engulfed in a yellow-grey blanket of fog.

There were comparatively few women on the streets and all without exception were clothed in the compulsory all-enveloping black regulation 'Islamic dress'. At the time of our visit Iran had one of the highest birth rates in the world and almost half the population of Tehran was said to be aged under fifteen. Right in the centre of the city all the major buildings were smothered with the slogans and propaganda of the Revolution, often taking the form of giant posters held aloft by scaffold-like wooden frameworks covering several floors. Any end wall devoid of windows was sure to play host to a massive and skilfully executed, mural: The scowling visage of the Grand Ayatollah Khomeini being by far the most favoured subject. Many of the biggest posters were lettered in English with 'Down with US Imperialists' and 'Death to the United States – the Great Satan' being particularly common. However, messages urging 'Death to the British' and to 'America's Israeli lackeys' were far from rare.

Tehran is such a vast, sprawling, featureless city that the only way I could navigate with any chance of success was to stick to the main road which in effect entered in the north of the city, passed through the main political, business and shopping districts and then emerged in the south. So, willy-nilly, far from nipping through Tehran via quiet side-streets and unimportant suburbs, here we were brazenly cutting through the very citadel of Revolutionary Iran in a conspicuous right hand drive vehicle sporting on it a GB plate and lots of English wording. Indeed, with the school's name, address and telephone spelled out in large red letters! As driver, my entire attention had to be given to coping with the frenetic traffic free-for-all and the distraction of the constant blasting of horns and banging of pane ls. 8 Thus, cut off from life within the bus, I had little idea of what my passengers made of the mayhem all around us or, indeed, of how in general they were faring. I did, however, in one chance interval of comparative quiet happen to overhear Slackie telling those about him that he thought it 'pretty cool cheek' to be driving past placards calling for 'death to the British'. I was inclined to agree!

Just as I was silently congratulating myself on how well things were going, I misunderstood a direction that Roy, on navigation duty, gave me and turned in error into a one-way street against the lawful flow. It was a quiet street and I might well have got away with my hastily attempted U-turn had not a small crowd instantly gathered to gawp at the strange vehicle full of pale-skinned European youths. The mob, noisy but not unfriendly, steadily expanded making it impossible to complete my common alternative to using the horn manoeuvre! A whistle shrilled and then a knot of some sort of neighbourhood police appeared.

The incident must have made their day and you did not have to be a specialist in human, or police psychology to see that all four of them were positively thrilled to have something out of the ordinary to deal with. Making the most of their luck they first had a lovely time inspecting every single document in our possession, for all that I doubt they had the English to make sense of any of them. For us, of course, a great flood of tension and anxiety during a long and tiresome halt, but this was as nothing to the heat we had to endure cooped up in the bus whilst our entire library of documents – both personal and for the vehicle – were eagerly scrutinised. At length, finding nothing amiss, the police next seemed minded to turn their attention to the roof rack and trailer, but instead, having noticed three or four of the sweltering boys had rolled up shirt sleeves and undone collars, set about rebuking them. Fortunately, the boys concerned had the wit to show contrition and, with us all now 'Islamically decent', they abruptly told me I could drive off. And all without a single word about our original infraction of driving up the one-way street!

Dividing the Iranian metropolis into western and eastern halves is an immensely long, broad, tree-lined avenue called Inqilab-e Islami. At least that's going by the street signs displayed at the time of our visit. In the days of the Shah, it had been Pahlavi Street and still was according to the *new* map we had recently bought at a filling station on the outskirts of the city. Yet, very confusingly, when giving verbal directions the good folk of Tehran always referred to it as Valiasr Street! Switching town and street names to follow the exigencies of political fashion and upheaval, I feel, ought to be outlawed by the United Nations.

It was early evening by the time we reached the very heart of Tehran and because of the searing daytime heat, this is by far and away the busiest time of day in Iran's version of Oxford Street. We were all taken aback by the bright hubbub, the jaunty crowds and the well-lit stylish shops. We were indeed astonished to glimpse through the great plate glass windows of the stores European style gowns and elegant outfits and a general air of fashion and luxury. Yet, high up on these same buildings the giant, stridently anti-Western propaganda was still there, and the grim portraits of the Ayatollah Khomeini still glared down. It was all very strange. Given my just about remembered experiences of wartime Britain, I had expected gloom. austerity and even sandbags and boarded-up windows. The boys, primed by their history lessons about the Blitz, had similar expectations.

Our pop-eyed absorption with this unexpected sight of bustle and gaiety was, in a twinkling, rudely halted by a very scary incident. A long line of army lorries had come into view, slowly approaching us along the other side of the street and all loaded with soldiers. A rabble of youths was trotting alongside this military convoy, shouting and gesturing with their fists and were obviously showing their patriotic fervour and solidarity with the regime. All at once cars began blasting their horns and pedestrians spontaneously halted to wave and cheer though somehow from the way the cars and pedestrians reacted, it seemed to me that there was a 'cheer if you want to stay safe' factor in it all. Then some of the wild youths escorting the soldier-filled trucks unfortunately noticed our alien presence and came over and started to rock our bus and beat the sides with their fists. The rocking soon intensified alarmingly and I was convinced they were bent on overturning our vehicle.

However, my passengers were magnificent and, as one put it to me later: "Me and Dave and others just waved back at them and gave thumbs up signs and I honestly think it saved the day because it made them think we were with them."

Fortunately, the traffic on our side of the street was still creeping forward in fits and starts and by continuing to inch slowly along we left the shakers and movers behind us though, for quite some time, the army lorries chock-full with soldiery continued to roar past. About an hour later and still well within the sprawl of this enigmatic city of seven million and still among heavy traffic, the whole urban landscape was suddenly plunged into darkness. Having experienced similar in Rumania, at first, we took it to be a power cut but then sirens began howling, numerous whistles sounded and all the vehicles around us switched off their lights. We did likewise and stopped close up to the kerb. It was obviously some sort of air-raid response and we had no choice but to sit still and hope for the best, each of us doubtless with our own private thoughts. Soon our straining ears picked up dull crumping sounds, resembling the noise of bombs being dropped some distance away. Then came a really loud boom right behind us and the sound of angry voices rent the darkness. Hard to believe but true, the furore had nothing to do with bombs but arose from car-to-car collisions as a number of witless Iranian motorists blithely continued their journeys despite there being scarcely a glimmer of light to see by.

Whether the sirens had sounded for real, or whether it had been a false alarm or even just a civil defence practice we never found out. I suspect it had been the latter as whilst researching our proposed journey through Iran we had been told by some knowledgeable RAF friends that Iraq lacked aircraft with sufficient range to attack Tehran. In point of fact, this assertion was incorrect and a little later in the war the Iraqis did stage a number of (not very effective) aerial attacks on Tehran using new Russian supplied aircraft. It should be remembered that during the terrible slaughter of the 1982-88 Iran-Iraq war both the USA and the Soviet Union favoured Saddam Hussein's Iraq despite the fact that Iraq was the initial aggressor!

It was approaching midnight by the time we had cleared the last grubby manifestation of Tehran's urban stretch and were in open countryside where it would be practicable to camp. It was too late to bother with cooking and in any case, we were all far too drained and exhausted for such a caper. A couple of heroes set to cutting sandwiches whilst other stalwarts brewed tea and discovered cans of lukewarm coke in the bowels of the trailer. The roof-monkeys threw down the sleeping bags and our useful little fishing stools and we sat in a satisfied circle, luxuriating in the fresh night air and in the wonderful – the amazingly wonderful – star filled desert sky. And yes, we did, rightly or wrongly, feel pleased with ourselves. We had dared the Ayatollah's Revolutionary Tehran and had battled our way through it and one could detect a sense of pride in the boys' conversation as they recalled the events of a very long day.

One by one they slipped into their sleeping bags and stretched out in untidy disorder, leaving just Roy and I perched on our little stools. I was somehow beyond being tired and wanted to just sit in a vegetative state and unwind.

"I'll let you into a secret, Roy," I began in a low voice. "I know this is a Moslem country and all that, but I do have hidden away a bottle of real hooch which I brought along for whatever special circumstances might arise. May I offer you a small sample?"

"And I, too, will let you into a secret, headmaster. I've known about yours for a long while and resisted all temptation."

"You devil, Roy! And I thought I had picked a perfect spot."

"A pretty good one but it rattled against the spare wheel and the maintenance boys heard it and thought the spare was working loose and investigated."

Chapter 11

Our next calling point was the ancient city of Qom, a very important place in religious terms for all Shia Muslims – in effect the Iranian equivalent of Canterbury. Qom is home to a great number of theological colleges and Islamic research institutes, many of them enjoying high status among the Shia and able to trace their roots back several centuries. At the time of our visit all the mosques in Qom were closed to non-Muslims and several had protective walls of sandbags around them though there were no signs at all of any air-raid damage. In two of the city's principal squares numerous army lorries were parked with anti-aircraft batteries set up all around them but nothing was going on and what few soldiers one could see were just standing around looking bored.

Though there was obviously much that would be worth seeing in the holy city of Qom, it was equally clear from all the military preparations that some sort of aerial attack was anticipated. Given that at Qom we would be nearer the war zone than at any other point on our journey I felt it would be sensible to move on as soon as we could.

Accordingly, having refuelled and bought some necessary provisions in the early afternoon we left Qom, heading south-east along the great highway leading to Kerman, Zahedan, and Pakistan.

Although the Shah had had enormous oil revenues at his disposal and had long enjoyed the fruits of a US-funded arms extravaganza, the Iranian people as a whole gained remarkably little from their country's dollar bonanza. The one significant exception had been the ambitious road building programme which the Shah had set in motion and the excellence of the major highways in central Iran was just about the only circumstance favouring us as we strove to traverse the immensity of Iran's scorched height-of-summer landscapes. For the most part, once clear of the main cities we found ourselves travelling along well-surfaced roads that were wide and straight and largely empty.

Ever southward and ever eastward, inexorably melting into the ancient lands of Persia, we journeyed on until sand dunes and blistering heat became the only dimensions in our world. Scrooge-like control of our on-board water had become both automatic and a vital part of our home-grown heat survival routines. To be up and away in the comparative cool of the dawn was routine number one: The second being the covering of all the sun-facing windows with wet towels. The wearing of nothing but a pair of shorts, a major defiance of the regime's strict religious laws, was made relatively safe thanks to routine number three: A rota of vigilant observers up front beside the driver to warn of approaching check points and so trigger some pretty smart donning of appropriate clothes. Routine number four was the daily acquisition of blocks of ice.

The idea of placing blocks of ice – about two breeze blocks' worth – on the floor of the bus as a crude, but tolerably effective, air-conditioning system had occurred quite fortuitously at a petrol station in Qom. There, an optimistic scarecrow had pedalled up to us, trundling a crude home-built cart filled with blocks of ice behind his ramshackle bicycle. My response to his begging us to buy his ice, especially given its filthy wrapping of old sacks, was to tell him to push-off, though I expressed the fact a tad more diplomatically. Even so, the poor fellow's skin and bone frame seemed to shrink visibly as my negative struck home. His pleading red-raw eyes bored into mine and compelled me to notice his emaciation, his numerous sores and his ever-twitching lips and limbs. Then, just as I began fumbling in my pockets for a coin or two to see him off with, I had a sudden brainwave. What matter if his ice was a non-starter hygienically? For goodness' sake, eating the damned stuff wasn't the only option. For surely, in bulk its mere presence just had to make the bus cooler. So, we took half his load, for which he charged us little and, poor soul, he then repeatedly called upon Allah to reign down blessings on our journey. And because all our broiling schoolboys opined that block of ice lying in plastic bowls placed here and there on the bus floor really did 'help quite a bit', from then on calling at the ice factory that all the larger Iranian towns seemed to have, became a fixed part of our daily routine.

The beautiful and historic city of Isfahan provided a pleasant and memorable interlude. Before Khomeini's revolution, most visitors to Iran would make a beeline for this city, intent on seeing the glories of its world-famous Islamic architecture. Now the tourists were no more and the city had suffered a sad decline. The appearance, then, out of the blue of a busload of young Europeans must have seemed the stuff of dreams to the city's hard-pressed traders and I had hardly switched off the engine on drawing up in the main square before we were mobbed by an excited, curiosity-filled crowd. Possibly regarding us as the harbingers of a return to better days, wherever we walked a train of suitors would follow, eagerly offering to show us the best sights and arrange for us the best deals. A policeman, poor chap, politely suggesting we park our bus and trailer where it would cause less obstruction, was shouted down and then chased away by citizens determined that nothing should spoil the warmth of our welcome.

"Isfahan is half the world" is an ancient Persian saying (it rhymes in Persian!) Reflecting the city's architectural grandeur in the time of Shah Abbas I, a contemporary of Elizabeth I of England. It was Abbas who wrested control of Persia from Mongol and Turkish interlopers and led his country into a new golden age. The truly enormous square where we had parked was the heart of this most Persian of cities. Once a royal polo ground and overlooked by palaces and magnificent mosques. Much of the square is bordered by vaulted arches which create a cloister-like shady retreat where traders gather and gossip. Among the cognoscente of Islamic architecture serious claim is made that the Masjed-e Shah, a stunning mosque occupying the southern side of the square, is one of Islam's most magnificent buildings and, unsurprisingly has been awarded the status of a World Heritage site. This gem is completely clad, both inside and out, with pale blue tiles that are Isfahan's proud signature.

We were more or less frog-marched to it by a small posse of citizens determined to show off their city to these 'tourists from heaven' (as one of them put it) and it was surely a great privilege to have such a famous and so atmospheric a building all to ourselves. We were there for quite some time. I found particular delight in the cool tranquillity of the courtyard gardens and I must have spent over half an hour just staring at the mosque's exquisite hundred-foot-tall entrance portal, feasting my eyes on a supreme marriage of colour and form. At one stage two mullahs, white turbaned and wearing black gowns over their brown robes, came up to me to talk. They were friendly enough in a rather reserved way and clearly wanted to know what I, as a rare visiting Westerner, thought of their revolution and country. Sad to say their very limited English made it near-impossible for us to exchange meaningful opinion.

Meanwhile, unknown to me, some of the boys were engaged in rather more intrepid activity. Invited, or perhaps inveigled, by the younger element among our eager hosts, they had climbed up rickety scaffolding (there were restoration works in hand at the time) to gain access to the roof tops of the mosque and so won for themselves a unique opportunity to see its famous cupolas in close-up.

Whilst up there they also savoured in privileged panoramic splendour many of Isfahan's architectural jewels.

A while later we were taken by our assiduous, self-appointed guides to another mosque, the mosque of Sheikh Lotfollah, which was nearby. In a way this mosque was the Islamic equivalent of a private chapel and so is without minarets because there is no point in calling outsiders to pray in a building they won't be allowed to enter. The colours of the incomparably beautiful tilework of this small mosque change according to the play of sunlight and where you stand: Rather as if you are observing a flight of numerous iridescent birds.

A brisk march to the other side of the great square and we were taken into the Ali Qapu palace, noted for its murals and mosaics and then, without pause, it was on to the 'Pavilion of the Forty Columns' (strangely it possesses only twenty!) before fetching up, to the absolute delight of the boys, in the enormous city bazaar. Isfahan is the focus of Iran's artistic and craft heritage and, despite the war and absence of foreign visitors, the range of goods on sale was breath-taking. I was particularly drawn to some magnificent blue bowls which were replicas of classic Persian styles and almost before I knew it, the ritual of oriental negotiation began. The shopkeeper who had cornered me was a small, bald and generously moustached fellow wearing a well-pressed cream-coloured linen suit and would have been perfect cast as Hercule Poirot. *Very* much to my surprise, indeed to my alarm, the pre-sales *politesse* had hardly begun when the fellow darted past me and locked the shop door!

"I see you have an eye for things of great beauty, Agha," he said, facing me and bowing slightly. "But the best, they are always too expensive for the traveller's pocket. Is that not so?"

I nodded vaguely, hardly registering his words so preoccupied was I by his peculiar behaviour.

"Englesi I think?" I confirmed this was so.

"If you give me dollars, I can let you have what your heart wants at a very good price."

So that was his game – or was it? My eyes roamed round the cramped little shop, seeing only a myriad of lovely treasures and *objets d'art,* all appealingly and professionally set out. The entire world, surely, for this bourgeois little man? Yet doubt and misgivings still had a place in my thoughts until my gaze chanced to fall upon his trembling hands. Then I *knew* this was no trap and that all the risks were for him. Under Khomeini, Iranians dealing in foreign currency were often shot!

A few of us found time to refresh ourselves in a traditional public bathhouse – always an interesting experience in Islamic cultures – before the hour came for us all to gather in a coffee shop and say our farewells to the dozen or so Isfahanis who had stayed with us throughout our time in their city. We had received every manifestation of friendship, one of the most memorable being the moment when one of our young escorts had suddenly dashed into a shop, only to emerge seconds later bearing a great tray of the sweet and very sticky little cakes which Iranians seem to adore. I can still conjure in my mind's eye the fellow's expression of total joy as he whipped round among us, pressing us to try as many as we liked. And I was lump-throated with pride when the boys broke into spontaneous applause as their thank you.

So well indeed had we been received here in Isfahan that as we shook hands and began to climb within the furnace that was our sun-parked mobile home, all thoughts of the ghastly Iran-Iraq war and of the antics of religious fundamentalists had left our heads. But alas, not for long. A sudden screech of brakes and tortured tyres abruptly claimed our attention. A pair of military vehicles had raced by and then, having spotted us, crash-stopped further along the square, discharging several armed men. Within seconds most of our new friends had melted away. The climate had changed and the brief spring had gone. As Roy slipped our faithful old Transit into gear and let go the clutch, I waved to the three or four Isfahanis still standing by.

"Safar bekheir!" (Bon voyage) shouted one of the sombre, pensive figures.

"Enshälläh" (God willing) called back some of the boys.

Chapter 12

Bar a few irrigated areas here and there, the four hundred and forty miles between Isfahan and Kerman, our next target destination, was unrelieved desert. As we had spent the best part of a day in Isfahan, there was only time to cover the first hundred or so miles before we had to find a quiet spot to prepare a meal and spend the night. We had learned the hard way that while areas of scrubby brown grass often offered the allurement of shade from a scattering of associated desiccated trees, in practice such spots threw up swarms of bothersome flies. The Eco cycle probably ran: grass…sheep…droppings…flies…ourselves and our food. So instead, we chose to camp on healthy sun-sterilised sand and rock by looking for a track or gully that first would take us a decent distance from the main road. On this occasion, however, the sand and rock floor of our desert bedroom was not as benign as we had imagined.

Up, loaded and away in the half-light of dawn, we planned to save time by taking a mid-morning brunch in Yazd, an ancient city three-or four-hour's driving from our overnight camp. Dawn departures without breakfast were known to Roy and me as the 'dance of the zombies'. You may take it as read that five am starts did not go down well with our young charges and we had to be pretty brutal to secure compliance. The first weapon in my armoury was a humble cassette tape: A recording, blasted out at full volume on the bus cassette-player, of a small German town brass band playing particularly strident 'um-pah-pah' music. Although this much-hated audio cassette was invariably successful in wrecking sleep and establishing a universal state of semi- wakefulness, it lacked the clout actually to drive the youngsters from their sleeping bags. For this final step a variety of methods were tried, some very possibly first devised by the Gestapo, but the simple expedient of giving the youngest boys official permission to torment their still stubbornly recumbent betters generally produced acceptable results. Shortage of water and lack of sufficient light precluded any ablutionary activity and from similar causes breakfast was unavailable.

Picture, therefore, the silhouetted form of the minibus in the eerie, pregnant glimmer of the desert dawn, absorbing one shuffling, stumbling, sleeping-bag-trailing figure after another until all our bleary-eyed, cavernously yawning youths had embussed. I take a swig of coffee from last night's flask while Roy is making a quick scout round with a torch (and as likely as not finding a treasured possession unintentionally abandoned) before I start the engine.

"Everyone OK?" I enquire, but there is no reply. The lucky devils have already resumed their slumbers.

An hour or so later and sixty miles on, the sun is well up and its slanting rays are prodding my inert cargo into bickering life. Complaints are aired regarding hunger, the need for a 'slash' and for someone unspecified to move his sodding elbow from the protester's crotch.

"I think a ten-minute stop is called for, Roy."

"Better wait until there is some cover."

He has a point. For all the obvious reasons, a dozen people 'going for a stroll with the roll' cannot decently do so in territory as open as an airfield. About a mile ahead the road appeared to snake through an area of rocky outcrops which would be ideal.

"Hang on lads," said Roy, twisting round in response to a considerable amount of noise and commotion. "We'll be stopping any minute now."

The disturbance, however, grew worse and became so pronounced that I could feel it through the steering.

"For goodness' sake," I protested crossly, "how can I drive with all this going on? Pipe down and sit still."

"Sir, sir, stop quickly," chorused several urgent voices. "There's an animal or something under the seats."

11 Naturally some boys sail as close to the wind as they dare in terms of language. Schoolboys invariably think crude language is more grown-up and so never stop compulsively probing their teachers' limits of tolerance, especially in less formal situations. Every now and again the cubs go too far and the lion is obliged to swipe his paw. There is a yelp of pain and the limits are re-established. Until next time.

I glanced in the mirror but as luck would have it there was a giant tanker truck on my tail and closing up fast. It was the first vehicle I had seen for a while and I cursed it for choosing now of all times to appear. Big US-style trucks driven by heaven- next-stop Iranians half-asleep from heat and fatigue were a common peril on Iran's highways and had to be treated with the sort of circumspection a wise hunter gives a charging rhino. I flashed the rear-facing camping spotlight the bus carried to alert the tanker driver and signalled I was ready to be overtaken.

"Wait until this truck has passed," I called, exchanging a hope-they-aren't-having-me-on glance with Roy.

"Oh sir, be quick sir. There really is..." The plaintiff's plea had been cut short by an anguished yell but by now I'd already started slowing down to pull off the road.

First generation minibuses were really converted vans and passenger access was through doors at the rear which, for safety, generally had to be released from the outside. I switched off the engine and, after giving my customary warning about our being at the side of a dangerous road, got out and walked unhurriedly round to the back to unlock the doors. I could see all the boys were, so to speak, starting – block ready to leap out but if I simply threw the doors open and left them to it, in the resulting mad rush someone could be hurt from becoming tangled up with the trailer towing gear.

"One at a time and slowly," I barked, still cross over their noisy hysterics. Philip Cairns was one of the first out and I called him to one side.

"What's spooking everyone, Phil?" He looked flushed and embarrassed. "I don't know, sir. There's a mouse or something in the bus and —"

"A mouse!" I shrilled scornfully. Damn me, you're not going to tell me we've stopped just —"

"I didn't see it myself," he interrupted defensively. "But there's definitely something."

His brother Tom came up.

"It ran over my legs, but it wasn't a mouse. It had too many legs." He shuddered expressively.

"Might have been a cockroach," suggested James Gill. "You do get huge ones in hot places. When he was in Sierra Leone my uncle —"

"Probably a tarantula," opined another voice behind me.

"Did any of you actually see anything at all?" asked Roy sceptically.

Several boys vigorously asserted they had felt *something alive and* a couple swore they had seen *something* dash along the floor, but no one was able to be precise. This was hardly surprising given the chaotic state of the bus. Sleeping bags, towels, shoes and clothing of all descriptions, as well as plastic bottles, magazines and general litter formed a thick mattress of junk covering the whole floor and under seat spaces.

"Right! The only answer is to have everything out. If you'd only be more tidy…" I stopped. If lecturing would make boys better, then pigs might fly. I clambered aboard and started chucking things out item by item, calling for them to be shaken out and then properly rolled up or folded. I was soon joined by two volunteers better suited than I to scrabbling about under the seats. They worked well and in no time all that was left to do was to sweep out the final dregs with hand brushes. They had barely begun when I spotted the problem.

"Boys, listen."

"What is it, sir?" asked Philip Gaskell nervously, responding to the edge in my voice. Philip was small for his thirteen years and early on in the trip had been christened *Squeal* on account of his mousy size and high-pitched voice. His good nature and perpetual exuberance made him universally popular.

"Just come out of the bus and I'll show you."

With both boys beside me we crouched until our eyes were at the level of the bus floor.

"See it?"

"My God. Is it…it's a scorpion isn't it, sir?"

"Yes. And I must say we're jolly lucky no one was stung."

"Are they fatal?" asked Tom breathlessly.

"Probably not. But nasty and very, very painful."

"Sir, sir. There sir! There's another one. So there is."

Once discovered the hideous, four-inch stony-grey stowaways were soon disposed of and there was some agitated discussion as to how to prevent a repeat invasion. The boys accepted that, given the high ground clearance of the bus, it was improbable the creatures had scuttled aboard directly, leaving them with the uncomfortable conclusion that someone had carried the horrors aboard in or on his sleeping bag.

"You'll just have to inspect your stuff more carefully," said Roy, rounding off the debate in rather unsympathetic tones.

"I don't see how we can be supposed to spot scorpions if you get us up in the middle of the night when it is too dark even to see our own feet," countered Adrian hotly.

Trouble easily flared between Roy and Adrian. As I've remarked earlier,

Adrian was a bright boy but opinionated and Roy had not yet fully won the respect and acceptance he felt belonged to him as of right as a teacher. In consequence he was apt to put the older boys down, which of course in the circumstances is as fuel to a fire. I saw that Roy was furious at being so roundly contradicted and I hastened to calm things down.

"Well, I dare say you have a point Adrian, but Mr Woodforde is right. Think about this one. When we get to India, for 'scorpions' read 'snakes' and for 'probably not fatal' read 'fatalities commonplace'. I think I'm right in saying that about forty thousand people a year in India die from snake bite."

These observations stirred up a deliciously animated discussion covering everything from proposals for ingenious anti-snake defence measures through to unbelievable tales of revered and ancient uncles who'd once served in snake-infested Imperial outposts. Meanwhile Roy and I, screened from involvement by the comparative isolation of the front seats, serenely listened with half an ear and adult smugness, to the youngsters' fantastic debate.

By now the ice we had bought in Yazd had long since dissolved into grey slush and nothing seemed able to counter the effects of the climbing thermometer as we endured mile after mile of the desert road. The boys had eventually learned that under such conditions the slightest movement generated body heat and that the great essential was to sit – or lie – *absolutely* still. A hard discipline for such a fidgety species to acquire! Obviously, a high liquid intake was vital and we had with us a large, insulated container of orange squash for help yourself usage. Even so, the insulation had no real chance against such a pitiless climate and within a few hours the contents, already rendered unpalatable by the need to lace it with water purification tablets, would be horribly tepid to boot. The boys, as one might guess, had come up with several apt and imaginative descriptions for our on-board drink but none, I fear, were print- worthy.

The journey from 'Camp Scorpion' to Kerman took us roughly ten hours exclusive of stops and all this within a single day at an on-board temperature of around 50°Celcius (say 120°F). Bearing in mind that many parents are driven to distraction by the boredom of their fractious offspring on a two-hour drive in a comfortable car to visit grandma, the willingness of our ten youngsters to spend eight to ten hours a day in a blisteringly hot, cramped and Spartan minibus for a spell of some six or seven weeks appears to defy logic and stretch credibility. With teenage boys, however, any situation generating strong camaraderie is always a winner, doubly so when physical challenge and adventure are part of the package. Nonetheless I dare say readers of this account are still likely to be wondering how ten lively lads kept themselves amused for so long under such unprepossessing circumstances.

Without the slightest doubt, what most of them did most of the time was chatter! From mean gossip and ill-natured banter right through to earnest, erudite discussion on the meaning of life. Perhaps modern living denies us proper opportunity for sustained conversation: Certainly, today's educators seem to me to be obsessed with filling in every possible moment with laid-on, teacher-led, activities. There were many precious moments on our journey to India, especially round evening campfires, when the aura of pilgrimage and personal endeavour was real enough and I am convinced that it arose from our travelling locked up together. We *felt the distance* together, as it were, as a band of brothers.

Listening to music was, of course, a popular diversion and from time to time I would run a request programme on the vehicle's built-in cassette system, boys taking it in turn to pass forward their chosen tapes. Many boys had also brought along their own portable cassette players but with these they had to make do with earphones: A strict rule as the alternative would have been Bedlam. Oddly enough for a square with positively cuboid taste in music, it was a tape of mine which was the overall expedition favourite – or rather one track of one tape. It was entitled 'I'm a Gorilla' and came from Mike Oldfield's *'Platinum'*.

In 1984 electronic games had not reached anywhere near their present popularity or sophistication but someone had a device called *'Gameboy'* which was in almost perpetual use. Chess was pretty popular too, as were various card games. One of these involved what seemed to me to be painful, perhaps sadistic, forfeits yet, inexplicably, it was quite a favourite. Fortunately, my duties as a driver gave me a handy excuse for declining to join in. Finally, many of the boys read a great deal. An overland journey to India is surely tailor-made for 'War and Peace' or the novels of Sir Walter Scott.

Chapter 13

Although the road linking Isfahan, Kerman and Zahedan mostly ran through desert of textbook character, there were stretches where irrigation schemes, some of great antiquity, had conjured green fields dense with crops and fruit trees. These green oases of course made much better stopping places for taking a break than did the shade-lacking raw desert. Besides, a drowsy camel slowly treading endless circles in a palm grove as it brute-powered a creaking primeval pump was a sight worth seeing, stirring senses much deeper than mere delight in the picturesque. Call it, if you like, the chance to sample a world of timeless simplicity. We even welcomed the invasion of one of our picnics by the ragged goats and fat-tailed sheep of a skinny doe-eyed shepherd boy. The rich earthy odours, far from offending, became a precious facet of a brief sojourn in a world no longer ours. In crossing the vastness of southern Iran, we never tired of these rustic – almost Biblical – scenes.

Yet I have to confess that our best remembered roadside break involved no image of bucolic charm whatsoever. Instead, the visual elements comprised a concrete hut, squat and flat-roofed; and a concrete water tank feeding a network of irrigation channels. As for the non-visual, a mighty, throaty diesel pumping engine was clearly busy within the hut for a veritable Niagara of water continually poured into the tank through an iron pipe of impressive diameter. The final constituent of the scene was a lone Iranian, presumably the minder of the engine. This fellow, black-bearded and all but naked, was energetically soaping himself in the tank, making it his private Jacuzzi.

All this had been observed as we had parked up just off the road some sixty or seventy yards from the pump house and tank. The heat this day had been the worst yet and the hours in the bus long and trying. We had suffered two tiresome punctures that had demanded a deal of heavy labour under a merciless sun. The ice had long since gone and our supply of water scant and disgustingly tepid. Our listless bodies, incapable now of even sweating, seemed to be struggling against an atmosphere of enormous weight. So, God knows the ill-bred conduct which was soon to occur had cause if not excuse. I'd pulled off the road simply to let

Roy take over the driving and to give the tortured boys a five-minute break to unknot cramped and contorted limbs. There was nothing to do and so we just mooched about apathetically like pub crawlers waiting for opening time. Little by little the rhythmic roar of the diesel pump gained our attention and our bored eyes lazily followed our ears, successively taking in the hut, the tank, the discharging water and then, with the mental torpor of a sloth, the bathing Iranian.

"My God," cried Roy, the first to switch on his brain. "There's the answer!"

I'm afraid we did not behave at all well. I should have asked the man if he minded. I should have restricted the boys to two or three bathers at a time. At the very least I should have reminded them to behave with quiet courtesy. I did none of these things.

The sun-baked concrete sides of the tank were so hot that we had to slop lots of water over them before we could even bear to clamber up and tumble into the water. This circumstance alone saved our blameless host from the tsunami effect of ten boys simultaneously plunging into his bath. Nor was it a particularly large tank; no bigger indeed than, say, a normal household kitchen or bathroom would be, so with thirteen vigorous hygienists aboard, it was quite a bruising squeeze. The water was cool enough to cause squeals of merry discomfort and, as life raced back into enervated bodies, boisterous horseplay signalled that all my charges were recovering fast in body and spirit. Expeditions by naked and near-naked youth were made back to the bus, first to fetch soaps and shampoos; and then later for clothes to wash. Our hectic laundering, the first in many a day, soon saw great rafts of foam floating gently along the irrigation ditches towards the four corners of the oasis.

The much put-upon Iranian had bravely retained possession of his own corner of the tank from start to finish and at least our unbidden invasion had respected that.

One by one as we took ourselves and our washing away, we nodded our respects and gave him our muttered thanks. It was little enough and God alone can have known his real thoughts.

We found Kerman, which we reached the next morning, to be a large and rather run-down place, though the streets and squares were colourful and busy enough. What immediately struck us was the number of soldiers on the streets, most of them walking about in twos and threes and without weapons, as if on leave. This impression was reinforced by the presence of some with bandages or on crutches. In the Meydan-e-Shohada, one of the city's main squares, we were met by rows of small tables spread out across the pavement to form a turnstile-like barrier and around and about them was a forest of placards and posters. All this, it gradually dawned on us, was part of an effort to raise contributions for the families of those killed or badly injured in the war. As people filed past between the tables, they would drop a banknote or a fistful of coins into slots cut into the tabletops and sacks fixed underneath caught the harvest. In another part of the same square an improvised war memorial had been erected.

Poles, set into the pavement and carrying display boards, showed photographs of those killed and gave their names and other details. There were about a dozen of these boards and the photographs all told must have run to several hundred. Items of memorabilia – a military cap, a medal or a badge, a framed family photograph and suchlike lay close by on the ground or were tied with ribbons to nearby trees. Many folks passed the memorials without appearing to pay much attention, perhaps because the displays had been there for some time, but there were a few obvious mourners. One poor woman, a photograph of a soldier-son in her clawed and shaking hand, stopped as many soldiers as she could, desperately thrusting the photograph in front of them.

Most, with the impatience and fragile poise of youth brushed her aside: A kinder few, perhaps seeing their own mothers in the distraught face, studied the picture before sadly shaking their heads.

We hadn't come to these scenes by design but had run across them while trying to deal with our task list. In particular, we needed new tyres and tubes for the trailer but, as its wheel size was little used in Iran, we'd been forced into the frustrating business of chasing up, one after another, several recommended hard-for-foreigners-to-find addresses. This process meant trying to make sense of street names in Persian script; no joke at the best of times but almost mentally unhinging when the locals are supplying directions using the old, long-established names and the city authorities, who put up the signs, have employed different ones – theirs reflecting the diktats of the revolutionary clerics. In the end, frustratingly and very worryingly all our efforts were in vain and almost three hours were lost. All we could do was hope we might do better when we reached Zahedan.

I had not thought it wise to allow the boys to wander off on their own in this soldier-filled city but our presence as a sizeable clump of Europeans inevitably attracted notice. We met no overt hostility, but we certainly did not win the euphoric overtones we'd enjoyed in Isfahan and at certain times I felt distinctly uneasy. One such moment occurred as we chanced upon a rowdy crowd chanting their patriotism – and their hatred of the United States. Very luckily this particular gang didn't appear to connect us with the bogeymen of their diatribe.

Rather incongruously, a fair ground had been set up opposite the war memorials.

All in all, it was a poor affair, but it happened to have among its attractions a 'wall of death' motorcycle show. This was a something that few of the boys had ever even heard of and which no one among us had ever actually seen. A desire to view the show arose, as it were, by spontaneous combustion and seconds later, tickets bought and distributed, our whole group were mounted on the rickety scaffolding, cheek by jowl with dozens of locals, viewing the noisy spectacle.

The arena itself was simple enough with rough planking forming the actual bowl- shaped track perhaps some thirty feet in diameter and about ten-feet high.

"Where are you from, sir?" I turned from the roar of the horizontally circling motorbikes to find a pleasant, clean-shaven man in his early thirties. He wore immaculate white trousers, a neat polo shirt and quality shoes. To my mind he looked more Indian than Iranian.

"From England."

"Good heavens! And these boys – eight, nine, ten of them? Are they all?"

"No, they are not my sons," I laughed, interrupting him. I had met the son's assumption many times before in the Islamic world. "We are a school party on our way to India. That's our bus over there."

The man's English was first-rate and had only a trace of an accent. I was as keen to learn his story as he is ours and almost before I knew it, we had all been invited, pressed and urged indeed, to meet at his house to take some refreshment. He sketched out a map for us, said he'd expect us in an hour and then dashed off – doubtless more than anxious to advise his wife what he'd let her in for.

Dr Nouri's house, like almost every other in its neighbourhood, was hidden from the street by a high white wall and an imposing pair of panelled gates. Whilst the street without was a wilderness of cracked concrete and dusty potholes shimmering in the heat, the world within enjoyed the dappled shade of palms and lush greenery and the tranquil effect of cool blue tiles and bright garden flowers. A fine bronze lion lay either side of the entrance steps and standing between them was Dr Nouri himself, smiling his welcome. Having greeted each of us individually, he led the way to a sizeable and expensively appointed room already chock-a-block with people.

As is Iranian custom, the males were seated on one side of the room and the females on the other. For the most part, older folk were occupying the chairs and sofas whilst the younger made do with cushions on the floor. Our boys, to their credit, latched on straightaway to what was required but there was one unfortunate exception. Philip Gaskell, normally as alert and sharp as they come, on spying a vacant gap on one of the sofas had promptly squeezed himself in. Among the women! The unintended breach of etiquette was followed by embarrassed silence, across which our urgent signals and stage whispers only made things worse, Philip perversely interpreting the fuss as congratulation on his initiative. And there, his impish face split from ear to ear in good cheer, he remained. Later on, the schoolboy species being the way it is, Philip's friends enjoyed putting him right and poor 'Squeak' came in for buckets of unmerciful ribbing centred on the theme that the only males allowed to sit with the women are eunuchs and eunuchs have squeaky voices.

Altogether there must have been thirty or more in the house: Thirteen from our party, Dr Nouri and Anahita, his wife and two school-age daughters, then their relations and neighbourhood friends. Small tables and trays had been spread about and female domestics plied food and drink. A good many of Dr Nouri's friends spoke very reasonable English and a garrulous atmosphere soon developed. We were clearly in the company of urbane, thoughtful and well-informed folk. Some of them had travelled extensively and had visited Europe or the United States; though for others Tehran was about their limit. All, however, were extraordinarily eager to hear about our experiences in Iran and to learn what we thought about their much-changed war-stricken country. I suppose the first thing I noticed was that there wasn't a *chador* or a veil in sight. Instead, a wall of shapely legs and attractive, fashionably dressed figures graced the chairs and sofas opposite us. A second surprise to me was the bold way in which the ills of the country were openly discussed – almost as if they were keen to tell the world that the hate-filled outlook of the Ayatollah Khomeini was not shared by true Persians. Broadly speaking, the Islamic Revolution was viewed by our host and his friends as an appalling tragedy. The intelligentsia and all educated Iranians, including the business community, we were assured, were vehemently opposed to Khomeini and his fellow clerics. However, our hosts explained, the war with Iraq had been a godsend to the revolutionaries as it enabled them to equate opposition to their regime with treason. The best hope, all agreed, lay in the growing working-class disillusionment because it was in the cities among the unemployed and those with little to lose that the clerics recruited their wild supporters. Life for the poor, we were told, had already deteriorated and such families were also bearing the brunt of the enormous toll of war casualties. Everyone, it seemed to me, was optimistically assuming that it would be only a matter of time before the mobs which had pulled down the Shah would next turn on the clerics. Events over the following thirty years sadly show how hopelessly over-sanguine were the views and hopes of our generous and kindly host and his friends.

"What do you feel about the Shah's role in the Islamic Revolution, sir?" asked Adrian, addressing Dr Nouri who was sitting beside him.

"Well, he's dead now, as you will know. But yes, a Shah – or a king as you would say – with constitutionally controlled powers in my view is the best way for countries like mine which have a long history and a strong social system. Having a figurehead is a good way of making space for various types of opinions and the different things different groups are demanding. Unfortunately, our Shah did not understand this. He gave only attention to his friends – these were mostly in the top parts of the army. He also listened too much to the Americans. They supported him with great amounts of money but that was just used for buying new toys for our generals. Very little was done to make life better for the Iranians in the street. Now the Pahlavis are no more I think we will have a republic for always." He finished by shrugging his shoulders and then, with a sad face, glanced round the assembled company and many shook their heads in agreement.

With the greatest of reluctance, by mid-afternoon I had to break up the party.

Our transit visas were now quite near to their date of expiry and it was essential to gobble up enough miles each day to ensure the Pakistan border was reached in good time.

"Why not stay here until tomorrow?" Dr Nouri had urged. "Then you will be starting out when it is cool and bearable."

The offer was hugely tempting but had to be resisted. Allowing our visas to expire would be a complication that didn't bear thinking about. As we took our leave, Dr Nouri and all his family and friends lined the pathway to the gate and, as if we were an honoured sports team leaving the field, all in turn shook our hands. Many also warmly embraced us. There was a great laugh when Dr Nouri's wife, Anahita, asked how much she'd have to pay for Squeak to stay behind and join her family.

Chapter 14

After the cool and elegant calm of the Nouri's household, facing up to the fierce heat of the mature afternoon sun seemed harder than ever and a conspicuous road sign proclaiming the end of Kerman city and the fact that Zahedan, the next concentration of mankind was 541 kilometres (say 340 miles) away hardly helped. Furthermore, according to our new friends, it would be grim desert all the way and by far the worst yet.

But there were positives and I tried to dwell on them. For starters and a very important element to boot, our faithful, elderly, high mileage, well-used and undoubtedly somewhat-abused, old Transit was still in business and sounding great – spritely even. A nice tick-over, water temperature just clear of the red zone and oil pressure still enough to move the needle a degree or two off zero. Well done Dagenham and well done the members of the Vehicle Maintenance activity option!

Another huge positive lay in the amazing sweat-soaked troops; seated, slumped and limb-entwined behind me. And, almost miraculously, they were still cheerful. Prone, indeed, to smiling and even to laughter. Their experience as welcome and honoured guests by gracious and generous hosts had of course boosted morale but it had done more: It had given a clear fillip to their self-esteem that both Roy and I could not help noticing.

Hour after hour I piled on the miles, every aspect of the driving becoming mindlessly automatic and the only dimension was dumb endurance – as if I were rowing across an ocean. On the whole the road was well surfaced and posed few problems beyond the unending curses of heat and glare. Yet even these were mitigated to some degree by the fact that we were heading roughly east whereas the hateful rays of the late afternoon sun came from behind in the west.

For a few miles the boys defied the mercury, chattering, reading and card-playing through sweat-stung eyes until ambushed by insidious sleep.

"My God," exclaimed Roy, awakened some hours later by sudden jolts and lower gears, "is this the road?"

"Not really. I'm searching for a place to stop and pass the night and this track looked fairly hopeful."

"Huh night?" Yawned a voice from the rear. "But it isn't night."

"Wake up Sunshine! And the rest of you. It'll be dark in an hour or so and you've a meal to get ready."

"Hall arranged and in hand," said Roy, hiding his yawn behind a polite hand "What are we having, sir?" enquired David Tite, evincing life from the bus floor. "Lamb chops."

"You should know," spat Craig aggressively. "The blood's still all over your manky shorts."

"Slack," sneered Adrian, effecting extreme distaste, "you're simply disgusting."

"Well, I like that! If I hadn't carried them what…"

"All right, all right, just pipe down all of you," ordered Roy.

"You know, this spot looks just the ticket," I cut in, taking advantage of an instant's silence. "You think it's OK, Roy?"

"Flat and a decent distance from the main road. No point in dragging the trailer over more stones than we need. Yes, it's OK by me."

"But there's no stream and no grass!" protested an unidentified idiot somewhere behind me. A plaintive wail and a loud 'ouch' rose above the hoots of chorused derision.

"If you can find water around here," said Roy heavily, turning round. "I would suggest you write to the Iranian government and claim a massive great reward."

I switched off the engine, suddenly wondering if there was another career I might pursue.

The gang set up camp with their usual brisk efficiency, albeit on this occasion accompanied by a spate of bickering. For some reason just now most of them seemed to have it in for David Tite but I felt too jaded to intervene. He would survive! As far as I was concerned, the meal was all that mattered and this, I listlessly observed, Roy and the two duty cooks, had nicely underway. I wandered over to the bus and got one of the boys to climb up and hand down my folding 'director's chair', which we carried in addition to the small fishing stools and some lightweight collapsible tables. Given the great many wholly necessary things we had to transport with us, a chair, tables and lots of stools might appear a tad over the top. Absolutely not! Believe me, no matter what background boys come from, if the eating arrangements are left in their hands standards quickly fall to a level that would embarrass a wolf pack. Indeed, experience had long since taught me that when obliged to *sit* to take their meals, boys as an animal species then invariably fell back upon the civilised ways of home. A further and equally important point in my view and well worth noting, is that meals taken seated and properly set out somehow give far more nutritionally and are much more satisfying than are stand up and grab improvisations around the stove.

The meal over, after the terrible heat of the day it was wonderful just to relax a few moments and stare across the desert. Little by little the huge red globe of the sun was sliding earthwards and, in a minute, or two would slip behind the purple-black mountains that still shimmered in the tortured air. Roy, like the good fellow he was, was busy chivvying along the washers-up and rightly urging them to be sparing in their use of water. Most of the rest of the boys were engaged in the ritual of argument and abuse that was the normal precursor to any ball game they were about to play. Abruptly the kettle on the big stove burst into shrill song and Tom, rather unnecessarily, shouted at the top of his voice that the kettle had boiled.

"Would you like a cup of coffee, sir?" he asked in more civilised tones, coming up to my chair.

"Yes I would, Tom. That's kind of you. I should think Mr Woodforde would like one too."

All things considered, the meal this evening had been a pretty decent one and the lamb and goat chops, which we'd purchased at the meat market during our time in Kerman, had been astonishingly good. As our resident wise-cracker, David Tite, had put it in reference to the market's non-existent hygiene: "I was sure the meat would be good, sir. After all, how could forty thousand flies all be wrong?"

I was a most happy fellow just at this moment. The great desert was now stirringly beautiful and the sky above it, a divine palette of pinks and blues and reds. Could the boys, shirtless and glistening with sweat, be golden gods engaged in some epic conflict? They almost seemed so as their moving forms continually scattered the spears of the dying sun into starbursts of blinding brilliance.

"Fancy a night-cap, Roy?" He, too, with his trimmed black beard and young scrum-fit bulk seemed suitably Homeric.

"Twist my arm! Oh, don't get up," he added with a satisfied smile, as I made to shift from my chair. "I know its new hiding place. By the way, where are we exactly?"

"You are supposed to be the geographer," I teased.

"You were doing the driving."

"Well, we've covered near on three hundred and thirty kilometres since Kerman and we've therefore still got at least two hundred more to Zahedan."

"So, this spot's about as remote as it can get?"

"Yes, you could say that. And it'll be just about as silent, now they're quitting their football. How they can see to play in this light beats me, not to mention where they get the energy."

"Youth does it, headmaster. Youth."

"Please sir."

"Ah hello Jason…Bloody hell!"

An avalanche of light and noise had suddenly erupted and was smashing towards us, drowning our senses in a confusion of headlights, engine roar and gunfire. In an instinctive reaction I had thrown myself aside, sweeping up young Jason Wright as I did so. Not until we both had untangled ourselves and regained our feet did my brain even begin to take in the wider picture. A large pickup truck, headlights ablaze, having thrust itself at high speed into our camp circle, had drawn up in an explosion of flying stones and screeching brakes. A searchlight on the cab roof had then scythed round, picking out a succession of stupefied faces and grotesque stop-motion figures. Half a dozen men, their faces half-hidden by scarves and brandishing the weapons they had been firing wildly into the sky, now jumped down and two others, both bearded, emerged from the pickup cab. There was a shout or two and before we knew it, we found ourselves being corralled towards our own minibus, some of the boys walking with their hands up like prisoners of war.

There was no question of our deciding to do as we were told, or indeed of deciding anything at all. We were all so utterly thunderstruck and so completely taken by surprise, that the concept of decision simply had no place. In truth, our shared state of total shock must have made it instinctive for us to come together and in doing so fortune favoured us. I say this because had we resisted, I am sure we would have fallen victim to the fire-first-and-enquire-later mentality of our assailants.

A stroppy young fellow, slightly built and sporting a wispy beard and military fatigues, began barking orders and in response his gang, thrusting their guns crosswise against our chests, roughly forced us hard back against the side of our bus. Oddly enough, the aggressive high-handedness of this action and its crudely intimidating nature served both to revive my wits and stir my temper.

"What the hell's going on?" I demanded, sounding according to Roy's later account, as if I'd just walked into an unruly class. At all events, at once I became the focus of attention.

"You speak English?" exclaimed the man who'd been shouting all the orders. He had run up to me and was now very belligerently thrusting his face within an inch of mine.

"Yes…er…yes," I spluttered. "All of us are British."

"British? *British?*" He was clearly astounded and ran his eyes from one boy to another, onto our vehicle and over the things we'd left lying about. In the long brittle silence, which followed and under the harsh glare of their searchlight, we must all have looked like actors in some surrealist drama.

Then at length, pursing his lips and nodding his head slightly, "Yesyou are British," he breathed. He paused thoughtfully for a while and then perceptibly relaxed.

"Do you know Nottingham?" he abruptly asked.

It was my turn to be astounded. *"Nottingham?* You mean Robin Hood? I added inanely."

"I know Nottingham. I study in Nottingham. I am there in study of engineering two years. I also know story Robin Hood. But then is come the Islamic Revolution and I go home here. Well, not here but Tehran. Then later I have work with the Islamic Guards and come here."

All at once a wave of relief passed over me. I had already concluded that we'd been jumped by the notorious Revolutionary Guards, something even honest Muslims would have dreaded, but now that we could make ourselves understood I felt confident that in the end all would be well.

"Well, if you've lived in England, you'll know all about tea. What would you say to a cup right now?"

He didn't answer and still looked totally shocked but, like a man calling off his dogs, he shouted a couple of sentences and his companions started to slink away back to their vehicle.

"Tom," I called. "Fill the big kettle right up and make tea for our visitors." His face was a picture I shall never forget!

The Revolutionary Guards had emerged during Iran's Islamic revolution in the winter of 1978-79 when the Shah was overthrown and the Ayatollah Khomeini had established his clergy-led fundamentalist Shiite state. The Revolutionary Guards, or *Komite* as they were also known, very quickly made it their business to uphold every last jot of revolutionary fervour and took upon themselves a host of arbitrary powers. They were widely feared and can best be described as half religious police and half secret police, a combination, if you like, of the Spanish Inquisition and the Gestapo. The Revolutionary Guards were in the main recruited from student-age zealots, people usually recognisable by their short stubby beards, black collarless shirts and green fatigues. Their favourite pieces of kit were Nissan pickup trucks and, of course, submachine-guns.

Once the man from Nottingham had settled down with his cup of tea, he introduced himself as *Mister* Sarmadi. The basic courtesies satisfied, I quickly went on to explain who we were and how we came to be in Iran and, of course, what we were doing camping in the middle of its great eastern desert. I was not blind to the advantages of giving this gang of machine-gun toting fanatics a little diplomatic lubrication, so I laid it on pretty thick about our keenness to see Iran's architectural glories and such like. In due course I ventured so far as to raise the subject of the alarming way the Guards had come into our camp, but Mr Sarmadi was in no way apologetic.

"This is a place with many very bad people," he declared. "The Afghans, they are near and there are problems for our people. For Iran. Many people come with drugs and bring guns for our enemies. It is our work to stop this. When we see you people on this old road, we say you with drugs or other prohibited things."

"And if we *had* been smugglers…people bringing things?"

Sarmadi shrugged. "We shoot. The bad people they have guns, so it is better we shoot first. That is why we do not shoot you. When we come near, we see no one has guns."

A shiver ran through me. We had been extremely lucky.

"You have good luck," he said echoing my very thought. He leaned towards me conspiratorially. "Also, many Komite do not like foreign people. They say many are spies. But I know English people. I like and make many friends. But your government is bad for us. It is for Iraq not Iran."

In the meantime, Roy had been busy dishing out mugs of tea to the rest of the Guards and some of the boys had attempted to open conversation with them. Perhaps this is the right moment to introduce the 'Yarm method for overcoming the barrier of language'. Over their weeks of travel our chaps had evolved a remarkably effective way of overcoming the language barrier when breaking the ice with local people. Their opening ploy was to ask one simple question in English: 'Do you like football?'

The word *football* was almost invariably recognised but, if not, a simple mime did instead. Stage two was to say: "I support Manchester United." Manchester United certainly enjoys worldwide renown as nine times out of ten the two words would be recognisedand faces would break into friendly smiles. The final stage involved naming various other famous teams from Britain, Europe and South America and, as each name was uttered, a facial expression would be produced to indicate the speaker's opinion of that side. In no time at all the locals would catch on and pull faces to give their views in return. As confidence grew, other body signals were employed. So, for example, someone could label Liverpool as *rubbish* by saying the word Liverpool and pretending to spit. Likewise, one could opine that Real Madrid were a mighty team by clenching a fist and holding one's biceps. Favourite cars were also sometimes discussed in this way and I recall one of our boys saying 'Polski Fiat' to some Rumanian youths and then pretending to defecate on to his hand. For all the obvious reasons I effected not to notice this regrettable excess, but I have to admit his clear, if unorthodox, language absolutely delighted his Rumanian opposites.

Now, I noticed, the 'Yarm patented communications system' was being used to initiate discussion on worldwide infantry weapons. One or two of our company, as is often the way with schoolboys, were remarkably well informed as to the merits of this gun or that and had soon tapped into a kindred interest among the Komite invaders of our camp. I rather think their self-esteem had received something of a fillip from the boys' obvious fascination with their weaponry but, be that as it may, for a second time the calm of the desert night was to be abruptly shattered by furious submachine-gun fire.

In all honesty I rate this second occasion as by far the more dangerous, for whilst on the first the Iranians had a firearm monopoly, at least the firing was in experienced hands and directed into the air. For the repeat performance of the machine-gun symphony, the Revolutionary zealots had lent some of their weapons to the boys, setting out cardboard cartons acquired from our stores as improvised targets and using the headlights of their truck to light them up. Believe me, the sight of a bunch of boys, most scarcely able to distinguish a safety catch from a foresight, firing umpteen rounds a second under scant supervision called for stronger nerves and a more optimistic outlook than I possessed. The apogee of my anxiety was to look on in helpless impotence as a lightly built James Gill fought a losing battle with the vicious recoil of his borrowed submachinegun. If I were to say that his four second burst of juddering vibration bounced him half way round the compass and he was only ten degrees from mayhem when, thank God, he ran out of ammunition, I'd only be mildly exaggerating!

Shooting of a more peaceful character followed when a 'team photo' of ourselves and the Dasht-e Lut unit of the Revolutionary Guards was taken, the resulting print giving the impression we had been pals for years. It was now time for our two 'sides' to separate: We hoping to enjoy a good night's sleep and the Guards doubtless looking forward to a successful patrol and the apprehending and summary execution of a few more enemies of Islam. In the event we were called upon to engage in one further act of positive fraternisation. From the instant of its arrival until the time for departure well over an hour later, the pickup's headlights and powerful searchlight had been left burning and it was perhaps not altogether surprising that the battery finished up too flat to start the engine. So, in an unselfish exercise of British fair play, we 'bump-started' Mr Sarmadi and his merry sons of the Prophet to set them on their way.

"Well Roy," I said, blowing out my breath. "Am I glad to see the back of that lot!"

"Certainly, an interesting experience," he acknowledged with his characteristic understatement. "I doubt that many of those who see such types arrive live long enough to see them and depart and depart cheering at that. So, I guess we must have done something right!"

Chapter 15

Despite the alarming postprandial incursion of the Revolutionary Guards into our camp, everyone apparently managed an untroubled, nightmare-free sleep. Indeed, as we broke camp and loaded up the following morning it was clear the boys were in a buoyant mood. As is the way with vigorous youth, they had reframed in their minds what had really been a very dangerous incident into something lighter and less threatening. After all, no harm as such had happened and so they sensed they could move on, dwelling on positives such as the thrill of having a go with the machine-guns and the kudos of having had friendly intercourse with real live gunmen. Youth is resilient rubber; age and responsibility make for more brittle feelings.

Despite a slick and breakfastless get away, two further trailer punctures hit us fairly early in our resumed journey and they not only took their toll timewise but completely exhausted our stock of spare wheels and spare tubes. All we could now do to make it to Zahedan was stop every three or four miles for the ailing trailer tyres to be pumped up: A discouraging and exhausting chore which the boys shared out among themselves with magnificent spirit.

In the opening chapter I have already explained our decision to take drastic steps to lighten the load carried by our distressed trailer. I also described the extraordinary events in the Zahedan bazaar that followed. However, though I mentioned that it had taken well over an hour to find a place where the trailer tyres could receive attention, I gave no details of what was actually done. Once I had dropped off Roy's sales party, I went on to refuel the bus at a scruffy, run-down petrol station where I asked the owner, largely by sign language, where we might get the trailer's tyres replaced or repaired. Making it clear that such small tyres would be absolutely unobtainable in Zahedan the fellow went on to recommend a tyre repair place which, he said, would be able to 'fix no trouble all machines'. A bold claim!

The purported technical establishment was housed within a filthy, sand-floored, windowless hovel and boasted next to nothing by way of equipment. A wobbly bench and an ancient vice represented the mechanical workshop and a couple of tyre levers and a battered old oil drum, cut in two lengthways and filled with vile-looking water, I judged, must make up the tyre department. However, once I had adjusted to the tunnel-gloom of the interior I was able to augment the inventory by a rack of used tyres and a dubious-looking compressor. A lean man, whose wispy grey beard only flourished in random areas of his gaunt hawk-nosed face, smiled a yellow-toothed welcome and his technical assistants, two eight-or nine-year-old boys, stared at me in wide-eyed wonder. All three wore filthy, *once-white jubbahs* and greasy *tarbooshes.* The man, one Amin, slopped around in a pair of old sandals; the boys making do barefoot. Amazingly, given the crude tools and primitive circumstances, this unlikely outfit managed – after a fashion – a successful outcome. Of course, it would have been too much even to *imagine* that **Amin** should happen to have a single tyre of the right size, let alone the two we needed and so it proved, but he came up with an idea I had last seen applied in the backwoods of remotest South America. Essentially the process involves making one just about useable tyre from two ruined ones. Honestly! By great good fortune we had kept two of the earlier casualties, so we had four tyre carcasses and two punctured inner tubes. Friend Amin first set to work on the tubes, clamping one patch at a time in the jaws of his vice until the glue had set. As there were numerous holes to deal with, this was a long and tedious affair. Whilst this was taking place Amin's young assistants were set to work with a tyre carcass apiece, their specific task being to apply a rasp to the outer circumference of the tyre until all the tread and rubber had been filed down to within a whisker of the cords forming the tyre carcase. This job was plainly tough, unpleasant and exhausting but the two little lads stuck to it manfully.

We were now ready to resurrect a pair of tyres by placing a filed-down tyre *within* a damaged – very damaged – outer one, in fact reinforcing it by providing a double body. This done, one wheel at a time the patched tube and tyre were fitted to the rim in the normal way before the compressor was started up by the simple expedient of stuffing the bare ends of a sorry-looking cable into the sole electrical socket. Finally, the now-hissing airline was connected to the traumatised tyre and, like anxious souls at the bedside of a dying relative, we watched for signs of life. The tyre painfully stirred itself and then settled into a roughly circular form. Zahedan's engineering maestro next put the tyre close to his face, the better to detect any whisper of expiring breath. Satisfied, he subjected the poor thing to the deciding trial: Immersion in the disgusting water trough. Success! Not a bubble in sight – or was it that the water was too mucky and thick for any bubbles to escape? The second wheel was likewise proved fit for service. Something approximating to fifty pence was demanded of us and, after passing through a ritual of bows and oily handshakes, we took our grateful leave of Amin, the man who had 'fixed no trouble' our poor trailer.

When, soon after, as already told, we fled Zahedan's townscape of low, flat roofed mud-brick squalor and headed north-eastward towards the Pakistan border, it was at the high point of the daily temperature cycle and the road ahead was barely discernible in the shimmering air. At times mirages, always of lakes or buildings and never of palm trees, would form only to evaporate a short while later as the horizon subtly changed. We met very few vehicles and these approached as ghost trucks, taxing one's credibility until they coalesced when a few yards off, as does a projector image suddenly snapping into focus. A long line of trudging loaded camels was passed at one point, making us feel like aliens in a time-lost world. Eventually a small building appeared ahead which somehow, in an undefinable way, seemed to differ from the usual ethereal visions and then I saw blurred figures standing in the road.

"Right chaps. first checkpoint coming up. Sleeves rolled down; collars buttoned. No laughing or anything to upset them."

Torpor transformed into tension and even Roy's sorting and ordering of the passports sounded ludicrously sinister. Three soldiers stand spaced out across the road, their weapons at the ready and faces grim and unsmiling. Twenty yards to go and a fourth, with sergeant's stripes, slouches out of the guardhouse, and lowers the barrier pole.

"They want us out," said Roy, pointing to a soldier impatiently beckoning us.

To my surprise they hardly glanced at the passports Roy held out to them and waved me away when I was about to present them with the thick folder of vehicle documents. Instead, two of them boarded the bus and roughly rummaged around under the seats. They were soon out again, removing their helmets and wiping away their sweat. The sergeant pointed to the trailer and I hastened to open it for his inspection, his soldiers in the meantime had lent their rifles against the side of the bus and were lighting cigarettes.

Of all the stuff in the trailer, only the remaining tins of food seemed to command the sergeant's interest.

"Dis?" he queried, pointing to a tin of chicken supreme.

Imagining he wanted to know the nature of the contents and therefore that he was focussing on our recent misdoings in Zahedan, my heart leapt and my mouth went dry.

"Dis?" He repeated. "For me!" His finger pointed towards his own chest. He smiled encouragingly. The penny then dropped as I realised, he was asking for it as a gift. What a relief! That he was asking for the tin as a gift was wonderful because it meant he could not have orders to detain us. If that had been the case, it was more than likely he would have simply helped himself. Within half a minute the barrier pole had been raised and, to a cheery nod from the sergeant, we had passed check point number one and were again on our way.

There were two more road check points before we reached the frontier, but they occasioned no scares and were a bagatelle. It was beginning to get dark by the time we arrived at the actual frontier and were positioned to begin the checks and procedures which, when completed, would allow us to pass out of Iran. Customs, the Army, the Police, the Immigration Ministry and the Komite all had a finger in the process and their own demands to make but all went remarkably smoothly even if it was exasperatingly tedious.

"Everything done," smiled Roy triumphantly as he dumped his pile of passports and papers on top of the dashboard. "However," he added as he climbed aboard, "they say we have to wait for an escort."

"Escort? What escort?"

"I don't know. That's what they said."

"I don't understand it. I hope they haven't got something nasty to throw at us after all. Escort? Escort to where?"

We were soon to know. A young army officer came up to us.

"Tell your people to get into your bus," he called cheerfully. "They must not leave it until you come into Pakistan. Please you wait. We have a problem with our car, but it will be good in a little time. Then you must follow us. You must go where we go. You understand?"

Of course I understood. At any rate on the face of it I did, but something about the whole palaver made me hesitant. Over the years I had crossed dozens of 'tricky' borders, but I had never yet been subjected to an escort.

"Yes, I understand," I replied. "But what is the escort for? Doesn't that road," I said, pointing, "go direct to Pakistan?"

"No, it is closed. We go other way. But you must keep with us. If you do not it is very dangerous. We pass…yes, we pass…you call *mines,* no? The bombs in the ground, yes?" He threw his hands in the air and shouted: "Boom!"

"Yes, we call them mines," I confirmed absently, my mind racing through a dozen thoughts. I badly needed time to consider this alarming development. But his instructions and warnings delivered, he had instantly taken himself off and we had no choice but to accept the situation. Just as we were all settled in the bus and ready, a battered open-topped jeep, belching clouds of blue-black smoke appeared alongside. "Remember," yelled the officer above the clatter of its misfiring, revving engine, "you go where we go." He framed his hands and thrust them forward which I took to mean we were to follow exactly in their wheel tracks.

With that he, his wild Fidel Castro look-alike driver and two other grinning soldiers, raced off.

"Boys," I called urgently. "Listen, I think we have to cross a minefield. We must follow the jeep exactly to be safe."

I knew before I'd finished saying it that my explanation was ridiculously scant, but it was all there was time for. There was an instant paroxysm of comment and question to which it was impossible to respond.

"Please," I shouted. "Can you not be silent? I need to concentrate."

Doubtless self-interest played a part, but the response was instant and we were one and all enveloped by an eerie silence and left to our own thoughts.

The army jeep had roared off at quite a speed and from the start I had my work cut out to keep up. There was no road as such, just tyre marks in the sand. Where the going was soft, having a much heavier vehicle than their jeep I was especially disadvantaged and before long about a hundred yards separated us. We drove for quite a distance more or less parallel with what I supposed was the frontier until we arched round eastward. In the main the track of the jeep was easy to follow but there were parts where the sand was marked by numerous conflicting tyre tracks and in these places, with only headlamp illumination to help in the failing daylight, it was nerve-wracking having to select virtually instantly which to use. Suddenly the jeep stopped and then began to execute a very cramped many pointed turn – it being clear from the way it manoeuvred that its driver was anxious not to run any significant distance beyond the confines of the notional road. The jeep then headed back towards us, clouds of thick black smoke pouring from beneath its engine.

"Our car is not good and we must go back," yelled the officer into my open window. His engine was plainly on its last legs and was only kept running by vigorousrevving. The smoke it was throwing out made us both cough and it was terribly difficult to make out what he was shouting.

"Now you OK. You go to houses there. That is Pakistan." He waved his arm wildly towards some lights that seemed high in the sky before being jolted hard back into his seat as the jeep jerked into motion, disappearing into its own smoke and into the blinding light of the setting sun.

Once the smoke had drifted away, I could see the buildings well enough as they stood on a slight rise and shone almost golden in the shafts of evening light.

Nonetheless I did not drive forward. The low sun right behind our bus was now casting a long, black shadow of it ahead, making it impossible to pick out the track. Further, to add to the difficulty, the sand just here was hard and instead of a proper rut, any sign of a track was, at best, little more than a vague depression.

"I'm going to try a trick I'm told they used to use in the desert in the war," I said to Roy, opening my door and gingerly steeping out. I inched my way round to the front of the bus before lying prone. From this position the bas relief effect of mixed shadow and headlight glare enabled me to pick out the slight denting that, hopefully, represented the track. It seemed to run on dead ahead.

I felt strangely and totally illogically, secure once I was back in the bus!

"I reckon, Roy, that if we just keep those buildings on our nose, we'll be OK."

"Here's hoping!" he chuckled nervily.

As I slipped the minibus into gear and started off, my gaze firmly on the houses ahead, the enveloping mix of light and dark was surreal in its effect. Behind, visible in the driving mirrors, the sky was a fantastic blaze of red and purple whereas to the side and ahead dusk had already laid its enveloping grey blanket, into which the headlights managed only feeble penetration. Then, with surprising suddenness I felt the vehicle beginning to climb and next the headlights were showing a definite road with steep zig- zags just ahead. Each and every turn, I noticed, was marked by white-washed marker poles and this could only mean one thing.

"Look chaps," I shouted triumphantly. "See all these white-washed poles? That means the enduring influence of Catterick and Aldershot. We've left the Ayatollahs behind. We're in Pakistan."

"Welcome, sir, welcome to Pakistan gentlemen."

The tall, turbaned sergeant had beamed his greeting past an enormous R.A.F style moustache and through glittering crow-footed eyes. A silver-tipped swagger cane imprisoned in his left armpit advertised his authority and gleaming buttons traced the contours of his impressive physique.

"Thank you, sergeant."

"You come a very long way, sir?"

"Well yes, we have. We've come all the way from England."

"Indeed, sir! That will be a very long travel. A very long travel indeed, sir!"

His voice was warm and gravelly and each phrase, delivered in clipped staccato, always ended with his mouth slamming shut like a trap. In his mannerisms he was the nearest I have ever seen to the archetypal regimental sergeant major of film and fiction. He leant forward and put his head into the bus.

"Ah, boys! Many boys. Welcome to Pakistan, boys."

"What do we have to do in terms of entry procedures?" I asked at the end of two or three minutes of pleasantries. We'd stopped at the barrier pole of a small block house. Two soldiers with shouldered rifles stood behind the sergeant at a respectful distance.

"Oh yes sir. You must do entry procedures. Entry procedures are at a very little distance. Have you weapons, sir?"

I shook my head vigorously. "No guns, no weapons."

"Very good, sir. Then you must carry on up this hill to Border Control. Those houses you see, that is where they have procedures." He pointed with his cane. "There are the Police and the Customs. My soldier will go with you."

Once we had made room for the slim, shy youth and his rifle and nodded our acknowledgement of the sergeant's fulsome farewell salute, we growled along in low gear up the steep, sandy, zigzag track. The Border Control buildings, which had seemed quite impressive at a distance, turned out to be – and smelt – pretty agricultural. The shy soldier did nothing to direct us to the right place but, limiting his communication to a sheepish nod, jumped out and promptly trotted off back down the hill

"Well," said Roy, rolling his eyes in exaggerated surprise, "I hope he enjoyed the ride."

The border police examined our passports and from them made long, wearisome entries in a great ledger. It was pitch dark by the time they had finished and the colourful western sky had disappeared.

"Next you go to Customs, but it is closed. You must come back tomorrow."

Chapter 16

"Tomorrow?" I screeched. "I don't understand," I added in a calmer tone, but still totally fazed by their statement. Its import was abruptly reinforced by the lights in the Customs building going out and the staff departing, the last fellow noisily locking the door. I turned to the two policemen standing beside me, giving them a 'what now' look. They shrugged, looked embarrassed, but said nothing. It took me a few seconds of hard worked, self-control before I reluctantly accepted that in no way would we pass through Customs that night. It was just our luck, I concluded, that we would have to camp the night somewhere close and return to complete the formalities in the morning.

My consequent simple question: "Where should we camp?" Raised issues of startling complexity.

"No camping!" Snapped a portly, well-moustached border policeman. "Here is military zone and so no camping," he explained in milder tones before earnestly adding: "The same regulation stops the grazing of animals."

"Wow, how awfully frustrating for us," chipped in Adrian, one of a number of youngsters standing beside me.

My next question, namely how far we must drive so as to camp outside the military zone, raised still more difficulty. A second policeman, this one with very noisy asthmatic breathing, promptly replied that leaving the zone was ruled out because we hadn't yet cleared Customs. Anyway, he added almost triumphantly, we couldn't leave the Military zone without showing our passports and these would not be returned to us until next morning.

"Don't tell me," I protested, "that you are saying we must spend the night in our small bus, all crammed together like sardines?"

The sardines were too much for their English, so I reworded my question.

"Oh no sir, sleeping in the bus would be camping." They both chuckled at the very absurdity of the idea. "Oh no sir, that is not permitted."

"Well, gentlemen," I said, trying hard to sound sweet and reasonable. "You know the rules around here so just tell us how you want us to spend the night."

117

This simple request occasioned a rowdy debate, conducted in Baluchi, between the two policemen. Two others came up to join in.

"It is better perhaps you go back to Iran until tomorrow," announced the noisy breather, in a sudden aside four or five minutes into the deliberations.

"Not bloody likely," protested Adrian with characteristic directness before I'd chance to answer. By now all the boys had left the bus and had gathered around me as I talked with the police. Other voices, equally forthright, were added. A loud guffaw and a raspberry rounded off passenger opinion.

"It is impossible," I answered in smooth, regretful tones. "Our Iranian visas have been cancelled."

The bureaucratic flavour of my reasoning won a sympathetic resonance that, I suspect, talk of negotiating minefields might not have tapped. They all gravely nodded before earnestly resuming their discussion.

"What exactly is the problem, gentlemen?" I asked, pushing into their circle.

They'd been nattering for ten or more minutes and I was becoming fed up.

"Oh yes there is very problem. You see ven there is like this you can go to the hotel in Taftan. That is permitted and, in the morning, there is return to here for control of the Customs. Many times, this hotel is used. It is very regular."

"Well, what's the problem then? Is the hotel full or something?"

"No, not full. But since very few days it has burnt from the fire. But wait, sir. Just wait very little. We send to find out…"

"What's happening," demanded Roy, coming up behind me.

I let my breath go noisily. "We can't camp around here because it is a military zone so instead, they want us to go to an hotel."

"So?"

"The hotel they want us to stay at has burnt down but I think they're trying to fix up something else."

It was easily another half hour before the spokesman returned but when at last, he appeared it was with delight written all over his face.

"You are all with luck. There is only one bad man in the prison and so they can give places for you."

I hadn't the energy to make a fuss and wearily nodded my agreement on getting a resigned shrug from Roy. The reaction of the boys ranged from feigned outrage to open delight! One of the policemen was due to go off duty so, saving himself a three-mile walk, he offered to come with us and introduce us to the chief of the town jail.

The place, a couple of miles away, was on the edge of Taftan and comprised a pair of bungalows with heavily barred windows set within a wire-fenced compound about the size of half a football pitch. A hurricane lamp lit and hanging in one of the doorways suggested occupation, but fifteen minutes of shouting and gate rattling produced neither jailer nor jailed. Our policeman passenger, presumably feeling he'd done all he could, then abruptly set off towards the town after shouting a few unintelligible words which might have meant anything from 'good night' to 'to hell with you all'.

"Now what?" Roy asked me in a sort of 'check-mate voice'.

"My dear Roy, you've just asked me my very own question. I put it to myself all of five minutes ago."

The jailer, a frail-looking cadaverous fellow, eventually appeared about twenty minutes later. He wore no uniform, the only clue to his position being a bunch of keys hanging round his neck. He threw open the big mesh gates of the compound and signalled us to follow, bus and all. The fellow spoke no English but made it clear that we were welcome to use the facilities of the bungalow he was opening up. The other one, as we understood it, was empty and remain locked, leaving us with the comforting conclusion that the one resident 'bad man', spoken of by the border police, had already been released. Finally, our jailer, assuring us by signs that he would return at daybreak, apologised for locking us in and, using a few gestures, explained that if the jail was not kept locked people were apt to break in and steal things.

The interior of the bungalow was appalling in every imaginable way, the stench alone ruling it out for sleeping. Stripping the beds of their filthy mattresses and the heaving population of biting bugs they undoubtedly harboured, we dragged the bare iron beds into the open air and made them tolerable by covering their naked springs with our 'karimats', tents, sleeping bags and suchlike. Meanwhile the duty cooks got supper underway and we finished what had been an exacting and nerve-wracking day on quite a high note, our sense of comfort being only slightly marred by the appearance from time to time of small clusters of captivated spectators peering at us through the wire.

We woke with the dawn, the sun's dazzling rays creeping over the ground until every bed became a cooking grill. Some of the more determined horizontalists, grumbling heavily, dragged their beds to spots where the shade was yet untouched, but this availed them little, for within a few minutes the climbing sun again had their slumbering forms in its sights.

Breakfast came and went, as did seven, eight and nine o'clock.

"Did he say when he would come to let us out, sir?" asked Dave Armstrong. "No David, he didn't. I presumed it would be first thing but obviously that was wrong. Nonetheless, I imagine he'll be here any minute now."

But I was wrong again. Ten o'clock passed and then eleven. It was hard to know what to do. We tried attracting the attention of the occasional locals walking past the jail but all, genuinely or otherwise, effected not to understand us. I can only suppose, shouting in English as we did, we must have seemed like raving madmen for whom a wire cage was entirely appropriate.

By ten past eleven I'd had enough. I started up the bus and though tempted to use it to force open the gates in a dramatic mass escape, instead I manoeuvred it tight against boundary fence of our prison. Wondering what I was up to, most of the boys had gathered round.

"Craig," I called. "I'm thinking a couple of you might trot down to the village and see if our idiot jailer can be found. If you and Alan climbed onto the bus roof, would you be able to jump down the other side of the fence?"

The fence itself was virtually level with the top of the bus but each post was angled at the top and carried two overhanging barbed wire strands.

"Of course."

"It's quite a height and there's the barbed wire as well. I don't want an injury." He looked at me pityingly. "Just watch us, sir."

Rejoicing as ever in their own athleticism, in no time the two had jumped the eight or nine feet down to the ground and were jogging along the road towards Taftan.

A few seconds later David Tite and Tom Cairns came bounding up to me, excitedly shouting 'Sir, sir' as they ran. "Sir, there's a man in the other bungalow and he's trying to get out!"

"Nonsense! It's empty."

"No sir. Honestly, sir."

"Have you seen someone?"

"No sir, but you can —"

"Er headmaster." Roy had suddenly appeared at my elbow. "We weren't alone here last night. There's a —"

Tite let out a whoop of triumph. "You see sir I was —"

"All right, all right! There's no need to shout like a hooligan. I'll go and take a look."

Ordering the two boys, to their obvious frustration, to stay where they were, I followed Roy round the back of the second bungalow and, without a word, he pointed up towards the top of the wall. Just under the eaves was a shallow unglazed opening defined by a wooden frame with steel bars screwed across it. For a few seconds I stood still, a rising tide of scepticism moulding my thoughts until, suddenly and violently, the calm was shattered by a pair of grubby, grasping hands exploding from the black void behind the frame. for all that they were handcuffed together, they began a frenzied attack on the steel bars and the wood frame, already considerably loosened, looked as if it would succumb at any moment. I had little doubt that before long we should have a real convict in our midst.

I had hardly started to consider what we should do when, with impeccable theatre, our jailer turned up as pillion passenger on an ancient motorcycle. Both he and his driver were as relaxed about the prisoner's antics as they were unapologetic about our long-delayed release. Their answer as far as the prisoner was concerned was to wham the wretch's hands with a broom handle until, shrieking in pain and protest, the poor creature desisted.

"What had he done to be locked up?" we asked, forgetting in our shock at the violence, that English was beyond our jailer's reach. He nonetheless divined our meaning for he expressively sliced two fingers across his own throat.

Mid-afternoon saw us proceeding eastward across the desert flats to Nok Kundi, Customs cleared and the remaining border formalities completed in a positive ambience.

Indeed, if the brief football kickaboutbetween some of the boys and a few unoccupied police was anything to go by, we were among friends at this remote and little used link between Iran and Pakistan.

The road to Nok Kundi, a run of seventy-five miles, was unpaved and chokingly dusty and finally killed off our poor trailer. Over numerous stretches the road was in an appalling condition, mounds of drifted sand and huge hidden potholes threatened the survival of our bus, let alone our dying trailer. Some of these potholes were at least a wheel's diameter deep but instead of water contained sand; but sand so fine that it behaved like a liquid. These treacherous craters, filled as they were to the brim with sand, weren't at all easy to spot and on numerous occasions a wheel would drop into one with such a horrendous bang that I felt certain that it had either sheared off or its supporting suspension had collapsed. In these conditions the wake of dust we generated made it impossible to see how the trailer was doing or indeed to see anything behind us at all. In fact, had a great convoy of buses and trucks been sitting on our rear bumper I would not have noticed a thing. As it happened, in all our five hours of breathing the dust and battling through it, the only other vehicle we came across was the local Nok Kundi to Taftan bus. This we found stranded in a sand drift but there didn't seem to be anything we could do to help that the thirty-seater's sixty passengers weren't already doing. Accordingly, lowering the gears and upping the revs, I powered through the great mound of sand with all the momentum we could muster and still only just made it – to the encouraging cheers of the bus's passengers and of our own indomitable on-board dust devils.

"I'll tell you one thing, Roy," I remarked, patting the dashboard in affectionate relief. "We're giving 'Lepra' a damned good vehicle."

"If it is still in one piece after another two thousand miles of roads like this, I'll agree."

Nok Kundi, with fair truth and little malice, might be described as a dusty, squalid, overgrown village in the middle of nowhere. A Baluchistan Timbuktu. But it did possess an official government bungalow. These, *'duke bungalows'*, a legacy from the days of British governance, provide overnight accommodation in remote areas for travelling government officials and for others authorised to use them. Although not furnished (at any rate not these days) with beds and bedding and so forth, they have water supplies and certain basics – in Nok Kundi's case even electric light and a working fan.

Presenting the caretaker, a tall, imposing and magnificently bearded Pathan, with the access note made out for us by the border police at Taftan, he opened the place up, enabling us to park the bus within its wall-enclosed yard. The interior, an eclectic collection of various sized rooms, clearly had not been repainted, nor, I dare say, even properly cleaned since the days of the Raj. All the rooms were thick with dust and only a few had any furniture, this, such as it was, limited to cane or rattan chests-of-draws and wardrobes. Every item was in a state of near collapse and clearly populated by the latest in spiders and unpleasant arthropods. Still, toughened by our recent stint in Taftan jail, the boys, Roy and I were all agreed this Nok Kundi Hilton was worth a try.

Before we could move in, the caretaker had had to busy himself chasing back to their proper quarters, the children, hens and other members of his wider family who had understandably spread themselves throughout the bungalow in the general dearth of clientele. He did so, it seemed to me, proudly, as if the place was his own home and he was generously making room in it for us. We had scarcely carried in all the gear and supplies we needed for our night's lodging when the caretaker came to me to say, in his limited English, that a man called John, had called to see me. Astonished and curious, I followed Zmaray, as the caretaker was named, to the gate where a slim young man, dressed in a long white robe, was waiting.

"I am a Christian," the fellow said, introducing himself and offering his hand. "My baptismal name is John and I live here in Nok Kundi. I see you arrive," he continued. "What is your name? You and your friends are very welcome in my town. Our congregation is…"

Anxious to be getting on with setting things up in the bungalow, I cut him short. "Well come in," I said holding open the gate. "You can meet all my friends. We're from Great Britain."

To my amazement, at this point the caretaker started shouting at John, clearly abusing him and for a while tried to prevent him following me. He then strode off muttering darkly.

"What's all that about?"

"He does not want me here. He does not like Christians."

It turned out that this Nok Kundi Christian had a rather sad tale to tell.

Apparently some fifty or sixty years earlier Methodist missionaries from America had been active in Baluchistan and several small Christian communities had been created.

This had been all very well under the firm impartial rule of the Raj but after Pakistan independence Muslims ruled the roost and all the suspicion and malice, they had harboured towards these apostates – and their families and descendants – was allowed to surface. According to John, Christians in Baluchistan were having a pretty thin time and, if his own experiences were typical, then social ostracism, attacks on property and difficulty over employment all had to be endured as the price of sticking to their beliefs. In John's case his job as a primary school teacher had been taken from him and he now worked as a humble clerk on the railway.

John was clearly a leading member of the Nok Kundi Christian community and proudly told me about the house they had built where the congregation met. He angled hard to get us to go with him to see the place and meet the folk in his community.

However, I felt we must stick to our set routine: India was still a very long way off and, given the challenging roads Pakistan had so far thrown at us, we just had to confine ourselves to essentials. Besides, we were all far too fagged out for such a notion, a good night's sleep being our sole post-supper ambition. I could see John was badly disappointed and so to do what I could to fulfil the expectations he clearly had of us as fellow Christians, despite the scowling disapproval of the caretaker, I invited him to share our supper which Roy and his hard-working cooks had just got ready.

The last few miles into Nok Kundi had been a nightmare and we had literally dragged the trailer into Nok Kundi with only the torn, airless carcasses of the tyres separating the wheel rims from the road. While Nok Kundi might well provide some fodder for your camel were that your mode of transport and, I dare say, even a spare lynch pin should you be driving an oxcart, its only contribution to the age of motor transport was a supply of petrol in jerry cans stacked up against the sun-baked wall of a squalid shop.

"Headmaster," said Roy quietly as our meal entered the coffee stage. "I've been thinking about those rickshaw things that we saw as we came through the town."

"You mean those three-wheel jobs based on Vespa scooters?"

"Yep. Don't you think their wheels are just about the size of the trailer's?"

"Hmm…yes," I replied thoughtfully, seeing in my mind's eye the little rickshaw taxis and miniature delivery vans that we'd glimpsed both in Taftan and in Nok Kundi.

"Well, someone around these parts must keep tyres for them," interrupted Adrian Meynell who was standing behind me. He was keen on mechanical things and had his own workshop at home. "Else how come they manage to run them all around the place?"

We put the question to John, rescuing our guest from the raucous company of Slackie and Jason. The tyres, he said, were 350 by tens. He knew that because they came from Quetta by train and as a clerk at the station he dealt with such things.

"Just as I said," cried Adrian. "Same as the trailer. We're in business."

"John, when you said they come by train, do you know which garages they go to?"

John's reply damped things down a little when he explained that no one in Nok Kundi actually kept a stock of them.

"What happens is they send a note and money with the train and then what they want comes when the train comes again."

"I see. How often is there a train?"

"There is one every week so things can come in six days or perhaps in two weeks."

"Six days!" exclaimed Adrian in shrill disbelief. "That means waiting in this hell hole…"

"Wait a minute, Adrian. Just pipe down a sec." I turned again to John. "When is the next train?"

"She goes in the morning at ten o'clock."

"And it takes both passengers and cargo and mail?"

"Yes, she is mixed. When she comes back, she also brings water."

"Water?"

"Yes. Many places do not have, so water comes with the train. It is from the government."

"Gosh. Er…how interesting. Can we get tickets for this train?"

"Tickets!" Boomed several boys in surprise.

"Are we all going by train, then?" asked Dave Armstrong, frowning as he joined the discussion fresh from his washing-up duty.

"Of course we're not all going by train," I snapped rather unreasonably. "How can we when we have the small matter of delivering a minibus to an address in the middle of India? But we shall, given things work out as I hope, be putting the trailer on this train and meeting it in Quetta where, I trust we shall be able to equip it with nice new tyres."

Chapter 17

The bustle at Nok Kundi station was delightfully oriental and it seemed as if most of the people of the desert outpost were determined to play their part in the once-a-week Great Departure. I had towed the trailer down to the station on its flat tyres at a purgatorial slow pace, trailed by a tiresome mob of yelling brats and yapping dogs. The 'game of the day', as far as the local kids were concerned, had been to clamber aboard our squealing, protesting trailer and I repeatedly had to stop whilst Craig, Alan and Dave Hall, in an exercise of good-natured muscle power, ejected successive waves of laughing piratical boarders.

John met us at the station as arranged and having his help made all the difference. The trailer ought to have been loaded onto a flat car, but we had not provided sufficient notice for one to be attached and instead the arms and shoulders of willing bystanders manhandled it into an ordinary covered freight van. There were several proper passenger carriages up at the front by the engine but Roy and the five boys going with him had insisted it would be more fun to travel among the locals in one of the freights vans.

For ages, long after the official departure time, scores of people were still milling about the train, dumping their bundles and boxes and animals on board one minute and then, the next, taking them off again and re-locating themselves in another part of the train where perhaps a friend had been spotted. Railway workers walked up and down on the wagon roofs, trying the brake wheels and exchanging noisy banter with folk below. Vendors of twenty different sorts shouted out their sales patter and porters, without any apparent rational, blew whistles and bawled out orders that none seemed to heed. Barefoot boys, playing games of tag, chased one another in and out of the train or hid underneath it among the wheels and coupling gear. Roaming dogs and clusters of hobbled sheep and goats added the colour of their own voices to the potpourri of sight, sound and smell that enveloped both station and train.

At just turned eleven thirty the gaudy green and cream diesel locomotive gave out a great blast on its siren and carried on the sound for a full minute before jolting its long train into motion. Slowly, like honey slipping off a spoon, station staff and idlers, townsfolk and traders, dogs and darting boys, fell away from the train as it picked up speed. Roy, David Hall, Alan, Craig, Adrian and Philip Cairns, their faces split into ecstatic grins, leant out of the open doors of their windowless and seatless conveyance to wave an enthusiastic farewell. Behind them, turbaned and placidly sitting cross-legged on the wagon floor, were eight or nine Baluchistanis with whom Roy and his five boys would share their two days' journey on the slow train to Quetta.

About an hour later, we of the bus-travelling brigade slipped out of Nok Kundi at the beginning of our own Quetta-or-bust journey. At first, for twenty miles or so, we enjoyed a stretch of new tarmac road but soon it was back to the familiar moonscape of sand drifts, craters and potholes. By the time we were forty miles or more into the journey we were again back to long stretches of soft sand and, despite the benefit of fewer passengers and not having the trailer to contend with, the blistering heat caused our labouring engine to run within a whisker of boiling. Once or twice, I had even turned on the heater in an effort to pull down the engine temperature, leaving the rear doors open in a desperate effort to compensate. The net result was simply to trade an unlimited ingress of dust for a negligible change at the thermometer. In bizarre contrast, at one spot we had also to cope with sections of flooded road, thanks to a seasonal Salt Lake exceeding its appointed limits.

A little later, just as I was coaxing the bus through a particularly tricky stretch of soft sand, suddenly came the excited cry of 'Water, sir. Water'. Snatching a glance in the direction of Tom's pointing hand, all I could see at first was a group of nomads, complete with sheep and camels, camped among desiccated grey thorn bushes on a small hill about a hundred yards from the road. A second glance, in response to Tom's further histrionics and I was with him. Two old men, standing with a donkey quite near the road, were filling water skins at a primitive well and then loading them onto the animal.

The well in question was a *shaduf*.

The schoolmaster in me automatically surfaced and I stopped the bus and told my passengers to get out and take a look at it. They stumbled out like the shell-shocked survivors of a blitzed bunker, shirtless torsos caked in sweat-soaked sand and faces featureless masques of crusted dust. I was shocked by their appearance and at my failure to appreciate just how tough things were in the back of the bus. Their sufferings had rendered them numb and spiritless and there was none of the usual chatter and horseplay as they shuffled towards the well. As they did so, the two men and their poor donkey, almost invisible under its load, moved away a few yards before stopping to stare in shameless curiosity.

Of course, I ought to have guessed that the well's ability to supply cool, refreshing water would expel from the boys' minds any interest they might have had in its importance as a schoolmaster-valued historical gem. Up came the bucket, eager hands then raising it high before spilling its gorgeous contents over some begrimed brother until, turn by turn they were all restored to a semblance of hygienic normality. I had just pulled off my own shirt and was about to ask someone to do the honours for me when I noticed the two old men were shouting and angrily gesticulating. What on earth was the matter? Had some fool thrown water at them? The question was scarcely in my mind before things grew worse. The two nomads were now in among the boys, the one cuffing them and the other lying about them with a length of rope and all the while the two shouting and obviously beside themselves with anger. Thankfully the boys were too taken aback for much of a reaction and I was able to call them away before things had spiralled into something really nasty. Even so the two old men continued to rant despite my making every apologetic gesture I could think of.

Eventually I realised the two nomads were demanding that I look into the bucket which they'd just taken out of the well and I then saw at once what had so understandably angered them. The bucket just contained mud and sand. In our ignorant and prof ligate Western way we had given no thought to the well as a source of a scarce and precious commodity. Thanks to crass thoughtlessness we had drained a desert well dry and had taken for ourselves what rightfully belonged to a poor community. Of course, I felt ashamed and ignorant and made what amends I could by handing over to them one of our big plastic water carriers, but it was little enough.

Meanwhile the noise and commotion had not gone unnoticed by those on the hill and several nomads were now striding purposefully towards us.

"Into the bus boys. Quickly. It's time we were off."

They needed no persuading and as I slipped from first gear into second, I heard the ringing impact of a large stone striking the side of the bus

We received a second dose of righteous indignation in very different circumstances when, the following day, we drove into Nushki. Perhaps rather larger that Nok Kundi and, for all that it lay astride the main route from Quetta to Iran, Nushki was one of those backwater places where a single new face could rank as the sensation of the week. As we stopped to pick up fuel and stretch our legs, within minutes a sizeable crowd of men and boys had gathered around us, one and all from toddlers to grandads, staring with undisguised curiosity at everything we did. Soon the bolder spirits were venturing a word or two, a smattering of English emerging here and there, with some of our own boys already involved in tentative exchanges.

"Everything OK mister?" asked one onlooker, a teenage lad in jeans. Almost everyone else wore the usual baggy trousers and outsized shirt universal in Baluchistan. Before I could respond another had said: "Velcome to Nushki. This is Nushki. Are you America?"

"I know Engleash," said a third young fellow, whose face was already sprouting an Islamic beard. "God Save ze Queen! That is Engleash, yes?"

"Absolutely. Full marks!"

"Marks? *Vot* is marks?"

A slim boy of about fifteen, wearing an embroidered fez-like hat and a cream, high-collared robe buttoned all the way down the front, was being pushed through th press by a small clutch of minders. He appeared nervous and yet was shyly eager."He speaks you Engleash," shouted the man at his side. "He is best student in Nushki."

"He is Abdul. Very good boy," confirmed another, a balding man possessing a notable paunch.

"Are you from London?" asked the boy in a quiet, low voice. "From England but not from London. We live in the north."

"From the north?" He repeated, as if not quite understanding. "You like Pakistan?"

"So far very good," I answered, trying to keep it simple. The crowd had become quiet and were plainly expecting young Abdul to do his bit for their town. Little by little I gave him the whys and wherefores behind our journey and he, in short asides, put those near him in the picture. And so, the word spread until, I suppose, the whole town knew at least something about us.

Abdul and I kept our conversation going quite a time and when at last it dried up the crowd, as if the whole affair had been some kind of entertainment, murmured its applause. Abdul beamed and failed in his attempt to look modest. Meanwhile Nushki's more important folk were rolling up, obviously bent on getting a share of centre stage. A few of these newcomers were wearing European clothes.

"He is of the government," said Abdul answering my discreet pointing towards the wearer of big flashy wristwatch who, pushing his way through the crowd, sported obvious self-importance as well as several pens in his shirt pocket.

"Good day, sir," said a crisp voice to my right. I turned to find a tall, broad-shouldered man wearing a number of ribbons and medals on his chest. He was elderly but his military bearing stood out a mile and his khaki turban and huge waxed handlebar moustache confirmed the obvious.

"And good day to you, sir,"

"What brings you to this sorry place?"

I outlined the purpose of our journey.

"That is what they told me, but I wanted to hear for myself. Is your school a military academy?"

"No. I t's a gram…"

"It feels like one," interjected James Gill, appearing from nowhere and looking inordinately pleased with his remark.

"Good. It is the only way to make a proper man."

Feeling we were beginning to get ourselves lost in cross purposes I did not reply but the old soldier was bent on airing his views.

"What is your impression now? It is not the India we had before."

"You mean…" I trailed off, not at all sure what he did mean.

"Why did you turn your back on my people? Why did you go away and leave your friends?"

"You are asking why British rule came to an end? Well…" I dried up; a history teacher and yet at a loss to know where to begin!

"Look at those," he cried, rising passion in his voice and fire in his eyes, pointing at the man with the flashy watch and his companions. "Thieves all of them!"

Then the flood gates opened. The British had deserted their brothers – their comrades in arms. They had abandoned the decent people of Pakistan and had given power to thieves and deceivers from Karachi and Lahore. We had taught them to respect order and honour and honest service and had then given them over to vultures. We were not true sons of our fathers. They would never have deserted their…

He was shouting now and the crowd were beginning to divide into two halves, many coming over to him and solemnly nodding their heads in apparent agreement whilst others kept their distance and contented themselves with dark glances cast in our direction. My embarrassment and anxiety must have been obvious.

"It is good if they hear me. I do not care. Am I to be silent before thieves?"

I was eventually rescued by Abdul who came to tell me the petrol man wanted his money. I returned to find the old soldier circled by a rope of boys, English ones and Baluchistanis, their arms and shoulders intertwined as they listened spellbound to tales of high adventure in the old days, told in an ad hoc mix of English and Baluchi. A charming scene I shall never forget.

Abdul and I fell into further talk and I learned that most children in Nushki were too poor to go to school. I was amazed to hear that although school itself was free, many children were barred because their families could not provide basic things such as pens or exercise books. How I cursed my ignorance, for had we known, a campaign to collect and then distribute masses of such stuff could have been made a worthwhile feature of our journey. We did what little we could, leaving behind a fistful of biros and a small pile of abandoned notebooks and writing pads.

Some hours later and still a fair distance from Quetta, I stopped the bus by the edge of the dirt road to consult the map. I say 'map' but map in Baluchistan in 1984 was an elastic term. We had first tried at the border to acquire an up-to-date road map of the region but without success, the border police responding to my enquiry by pronouncing the need for a map as absurd given there was only one road from Taftan to Nok Kundi! We had no better luck in Nok Kundi or Nashki either. The map I did have had been obtained from the Pakistan High Commission in London but. lacking any topographical information whatsoever. it was next to useless in an area devoid of road signs. Right in front of us was a three-way junction, without any indication of where the three dirt roads, looking more or less equal in importance, led to. According to the map, if we were where we thought we were, there should only have been a simple fork. The desert had gradually become undulating and broken and over the last hour the road had taken us among rocky formations of ever-increasing scale until we found ourselves among mountains of daunting aspect.

I got out and walked a few yards to see what the compass said but the mystery junction, ringed as it was by towering heights of raw red rock, seemed to make the compass twitchy and it was hard to make sense of its readings. If anything, I decided the middle road looked the most promising. I must stress that the whole business was much more than an academic exercise in navigation with inconvenience as the downside of a mistake. For a start, get the road wrong in this terrain and we might well end up out of fuel (and water!) Absolutely in the middle of nowhere where there was little chance of meeting another human in days. More sobering still, according to our map the Nushki to Quetta Road ran within seven miles of the Afghan border and in 1984 the Soviet Union had over 100,000 troops in Afghanistan supporting a hated pro-Soviet government. Opposing them was an increasingly successful nationalist guerrilla army known as the Mujahedeen and much of the most bitter fighting was taking place along this very Pakistan-Afghan border – a border that by the very nature of its wild mountainous character was both ill-defined and subject to dispute. Whatever happened we must not stray into Afghanistan!

In all the time we had been on the road after leaving Nushki we had only met two other vehicles and these, both buses with enormous piles of luggage stacked on their roofs, I had tried to flag down. But in both instances without success. It would have been reassuring just to have had them confirm we were on the right road but their reluctance to oblige was understandable. A little while earlier we had passed a man and a boy wearily trudging along the road, miles from anywhere and had offered them a lift. The man, a tall lithe fellow, was an Afghan to judge by his appearance and the boy, a light-skinned lad of about eleven with arresting but horribly sore, pale blue eyes, I had taken to be his son or perhaps grandson. So far, though they seemed pleased enough about the lift, we had not managed to get a single word out of them. Now, I felt, it was time for them to make themselves useful. We had no end of trouble persuading them to get out of the bus and I'm sure we would have had a much easier time had we needed to eject a bull from a cattle truck. My two Afghans simply just sat, refusing to communicate, budge or even move a muscle. In the end, with the pre-planned help of two of my boys, I unceremoniously bundled the small boy out of the bus, whereupon the man, after shouting what I assumed was a protest, got out without further ado.

I, let us say, 'nudged', our guests forward until they stood in front of the bus with the three-forked junction right ahead of them.

"Quetta?" I now asked, pointing to each road in turn. The boy still said nothing, but the man gave a slight shrug for the left and right directions and a few guttural words for the centre. On that slender indication I started the engine and resumed our journey.

Chapter 18

Every mile increased my doubts about the road. Though from time to time I would turn to the wretched Afghan and point ahead and say "Quetta?" In a questioning tone, all he ever did was nod his hawk-nosed head and flop his arm vaguely forwards. The general trend of the road was upward and ever upward but within this there were miles of hairpin descents down to some valley bottom before a new climb commenced on the far side. Most of these valleys cradled dry riverbeds but some had fast-flowing streams and as often as not there was a ford rather than a bridge. At one shallow but unusually sandy ford I almost got into real trouble and only the united efforts of every passenger, the two Afghans included, pushing and heaving in the ice-cold water saved the day.

By this point I needed no persuading that we were almost certainly on the wrong road, the main question now being what to do about it. The map was useless and even trying to work out our general direction from the position of the sun was virtually impossible due to winding character of the road. I was almost on the point of turning around, only the thought of having to re-tackle the sandy ford holding me, when the road gave a hint that we might be coming to some sort of settlement. First scattered trees started appearing near the road and then came orchards and isolated dwellings. The sense of relief, after covering seemingly endless miles of wild, lifeless mountain terrain, not having a clue as to where we were or where we were heading, was quite extraordinary.

Then, straight after turning a blind corner, the road began to run between high mud walls and there before us were walking human beings. We'd arrived in a place called Burj and upon hearing this I became quite lightheaded for Burj was marked on my map!

Not that it was all good news. We were now way up in the mountains at almost seven thousand feet and only a handful of miles from the Afghan border. Equally negative, Burj had no petrol and a dwindling tank is a serious thing to have to worry about in such terrain, to say the least of it. The long and the short of the matter was we still had many miles to cover and much of the remaining distance would be over roads no less rough and slow. Nonetheless, by pressing on we now knew we would eventually meet the main Quetta to Charman road (Charman being the entry town for Afghanistan) above the Khojak Pass.

Half an hour later on cresting the last of a series of ridges, each one of which I had optimistically expected would be the summit of our climb, we saw in the valley, perhaps a thousand feet below, what appeared to be a large township. As no town was marked anywhere hereabouts on our map, I again felt close to despair. Surely, I hadn't taken another wrong turning? But how could I when we hadn't passed as much as a hint of a turnout, let alone a junction? Dusk was now fast approaching and the valley, already in shadow, was almost lost in the smoke of innumerable fires. The mystery town turned out to be a tented settlement of Afghan refugees. Most of the dwellings were lumpylooking black goats' hair tents, typical in Afghanistan, but in stark contrast there were also new canvas ones with stencilled lettering proclaiming which governments and aid agencies had provided them.

The effect of driving into the camp was like kicking open an anthill. Fierce-looking men and dour-faced unsmiling women stood up from their cooking fires to gaze at us whilst other men ran down the steep tented slopes, leaping guy ropes and boulders like knights on a chessboard, before fetching up on the road. Then, grimly purposeful, they strode along beside us. Whether likely to be friends or foes, it was impossible to tell. Children gathered noisily in our wake, several balancing themselves on our rear bumper, whilst ahead yelling boys frantically slapped sheep and goats to get them out of our way. Just at the moment when it seemed vital to have windows closed and doors locked, our on-board Afghan and his boy let it be known we'd reached their desired bus stop.

"The crafty old devil," I exclaimed turning towards Jason Wright who was sharing the front seat with me. "You remember that three-way junction? The cunning b-blighter! I'll bet ten dollars to a doughnut that he made out the middle road was for Quetta just so we'd give him and his brat a ride home. The actual road for Quetta must have been the one to the right. That explains why we've fetched up here among these damned great mountains."

"What will you do," asked David Tite "from the back?"

"There's nothing I *can* do, David. Go and open the door Jason," I said wearily, "and let's get rid of them!"

Our dropping off two of their own appeared to soften the aspect of the gazing, encircling, unsmiling Afghan faces. My ex-passenger nodded his head as he passed my window which I took to be a minimalist 'thank you' and the boy went so far as to give me a shy wave. I could feel my sense of outrage subsiding.

The road snaked its way among the tents and animals and among staring, proudly implacable Afghans right down to the bottom of the valley. Here, instead of crossing the little trickle that represented the river at this season, it ran along beside it, intermingling until the dried upriver bed and the road became one and the same thing.

"We'll not make Quetta tonight, boys," I announced. "It's already nearly dark and I can hardly tell the road from the river."

"Where are we going to camp?" asked Tom.

"Right here, more or less. It's no use looking for green fields, that's for sure."

It was to prove a confusing and traumatic night. I'd stopped about thirty yards off the road on a slight eminence almost overhanging the river. As we had not met any vehicle at all on our long drive through the mountainous wilderness between Burj and the Afghan cam, I was hoping for a traffic-free night. This proved to be true for motor vehicles, but the sinister glide of ghostly silhouettes as loaded camels, driven flocks and sundry pedestrians padded by, made for fretful sleep when sleep would come at all. We had stationed ourselves about half a mile beyond the Afghan camp but as the last dregs of daylight drained away and we ate our supper and made ready for the night, knots of curious spectators started popping along to gawp at the goings-on of their new foreign neighbours. For the most part they kept a decent distance, but bolder ones would come right up to the bus and peer inside.

'Americanzi?' they often asked in their thick guttural tones.

"No, Engelezi," we replied in cheery tones, hoping to keep things friendly.

A sort of singsong "a-ah" generally followed. A number of small girls started appearing amongst the spectators and even a few women. Here they were unveiled, simply having shawls over their heads like Victorian factory girls. Some of the men carried traditional *135ezail* long barrelled rifles and a few also wore bandoleers over a sleeveless sheepskin 'war jacket', these latter fellows looking very like *mujahedeen* to my untutored eye. The onset of darkness did little to discourage the constant relay of spectators.

"They even follow you to watch you pee," complained James Gill.

Then, to our great surprise our two former passengers, accompanied by a couple of pals, also made us a visit. The boy dumped a bag by the door of the bus, making it clear it was a gift.

"What are they, sir?" asked Tom, peering into the bag.

"Pomegranates, aren't they?" said Slackie, pulling out a fruit and holding it up for me to see.

"I think so."

"Sir," shouted Tom, suddenly animated. "Why don't we give them the eye drops in return?"

"Eye drops?" I repeated vacantly.

"Yes sir. Those in the First Aid box that we were supposed to use in dusty places."

"He's right, sir," chipped in James Gill. James, aged fourteen, was a bright lad academically and we had every hope of his getting into a top medical faculty in due time. It had seemed only right to put him in charge of First Aid.

"We've never used them," James continued. "They might help the kid. Just look at his eyes, sir. They're awful."

"What a damn good idea," I exclaimed, in part relieved as I was already feeling a touch guilty over my earlier dark thoughts concerning our passengers' honesty. The drops referred to were meant to give relief to anyone suffering sore eyes as a result of dry and dusty desert air. Somehow, for all the many discomforts of our long desert travels, we'd never resorted to them – indeed I'd quite forgotten we had them.

"We've got six tiny bottles, sir."

"Well let's give them three. But will the guy, I wonder, know how to use them?"

"We can give him a demo. Tom or James can pretend to be my patient."

Both boys effected horrified reluctance but seconds later, with an air of confidence I found startling, the three had marched over to our two ex-passengers – man and boy – and, hands and faces engaged in busy mime, launched their mission. A crowd, like schoolboys watching a playground fight, quickly formed and packed round the boy-medics, leaving me craning my neck as I tried to glipse the action.

Nearest was Tom, one arm cradling the Afghan boy's shoulders and the other holding a torch. Centre stage was Danny, his face a study in concentration, gently bathing a pair of anxious eyes. And there was dad – or was he grandad? His huge brown hands steadying the boy's head. Was I wrong to feel proud? Was it silly sentiment that filled my own eyes with moisture? The clinic certainly delayed our bedtime for naturally other patients materialised and by the time we had seen the last we had medical shortages across the board, to say nothing of a total dearth of eye drops.

Within a few minutes of the last of our 'patients' shuffling off, many of us were stifling yawns and preparing for bed. It had been a very long day. Most of the boys, as had become their habit over weeks of desert travel, would simply get into their sleeping bags and lie here and there on the ground close to the bus. A couple might, for a change, choose to stretch out on the floor or across a couple of seats in the bus but outside on a karrimat on the bare ground was the usual thing. I, as was my habit, would snuggle down in privileged isolation on the bench-like front seat. But this night I found the unending toing and froing of Afghans past the bus unsettling and I stood, leaning against the bus, gazing pensively at an amazing star-drenched sky. Little by little my unease increased. Afghan refugees had been much in the news this last year or so and not a lot of it was to their credit.

"Is the river OK for teeth, sir?"

"Teeth? Oh…er…I see what you mean." Tom and David Tite were standing by me holding toothbrushes. David was wearing a gaudy bobble hat. "No, not really. It's downstream from the refugee camp. Use the water in the bus."

"Are you all right, sir?" asked Tom. "You look sort of worried."

"Just thinking, Tom, that's all. The worry must have been the sight of Slackie's hat."

They both grinned.

But Tom had been perceptive. I *was* worried. And it took me less than another minute to focus my thoughts and decide upon a course of action.

Put simply, I was not comfortable with our situation. First, I missed the sense of security that the capable presence of Roy and the five older lads had automatically provided. I did not feel at all happy that these younger boys should be scattered about on their own even though I noticed, doubtless on account of the cold at this height, that two tents had been erected. But essentially, it was the presence of the Afghans that had me worried. While I was sure that most of them would be fine and, thankful for the refuge they had found in Pakistan, be careful to steer clear of trouble.

Nonetheless, as was common knowledge, hiding among the legitimate folk who had fled the fighting raging in Afghanistan, were various independent guerrilla groups referred to generically as Mujahedeen. Many of these gentlemen, to say the least of it, had a questionable agenda. I collared James whose chosen sleeping spot was conveniently right next to the bus.

"I'm sorry to disturb you, James, but I've a job for you. Would you get up and kindly wake everyone. I want to talk to you all. Do it as quietly and quickly as you can."

Within minutes everyone had dutifully appeared, most hugging themselves in the cold night air.

"Boys, l i s t e n. I'm really sorry I've had to spoil your sleep, but I've decided it will be better if we all sleep inside the bus tonight. Two of you will put up a tent on the roof and the rest will sleep inside on the seats as best you can."

"On the roof!" exclaimed James. "How can we put a tent on the roof?"

"Ah! It can be done, James. Indeed, the luggage rack was built with the idea in mind and you'll find the *Vango* just fits inside the rails. What you do is erect the tent as normal – there are holes in the rack floor for the poles – fixing up the tent by tying the cords and ropes as best you can to the bars of the rack. And, by the way James, don't let me see you trying to hammer tent pegs into the roof!"

"Oh sir!"

"What about the stuff that's already on the roof?" Demanded Slackie.

"It must all come down. Valuable things must go inside the bus and we'll push the rest out of sight under it. Perhaps you can organise that, David."

It was already late and everybody clearly wanted to get back horizontal as fast as possible, so the chores needed to get the new sleeping plan set up were tackled quickly and without the slightest fuss. Indeed, the boys were superb.

"One last thing," I said. "I expect you'd like to know why I got you up and caused this hoo-ha. Well, the long and short of it is I don't think this is a good camping place, though in truth we had little choice. We're very near the river and in this sort of terrain a dangerous flash flood, though unlikely, can't be ruled out. But the main reason is that there are far too many dubious folks around and I think it better we are all together. And I'm also going mount a kind of guard."

Far from any sign of alarm, their moonlit faces brightened with boyish excitement. "Do you think we'll be attacked?" asked Jason, his tone half thrilled and half fearful.

"No of course I don't. If I thought that, do you think we would still be remaining here?"

"But there's just an off chance, is that it, sir?" asked Slackie, clearly reluctant to forgo all thought of heroic events.

"Well, as I said before, there are too many folks wandering about for my liking. You see, with everybody already aboard I'm thinking that if anything arose, we could just start up and whiz off."

"Good thinking, sir," said Slackie, nodding his head and pulling his face into an expression of great sagacity.

"For some reason I don't feel all that sleepy so what I suggest is that I will stay up keeping an eye on things for a couple of hours and then I'll wake you, James and you can take over for an hour. After that you can swap with…er…Jason and so on."

"You're on the roof aren't you Jase?"

"Yes, on the left."

"Sir, where should we watch from?"

"Good question. Get a small stool and sit on that by the side of the bus but every now and then take a walk round it so you don't nod off."

"Can I borrow the big torch, sir?"

"Of course you can. I'll give you it when you take over."

"And what about having the machete? I would sort of feel more like a real…"

"Oh, I don't think so, James. I'm never very keen…well, yes OK. Yes, why not? I'll leave it on the top of the right front wheel."

"Sir, sir. Wake up…sir."

It was James' voice but all I could see was the glare of the torch. "What is it? And for Heaven's sake stop shining that torch in my face."

"Sorry sir. It's the army, sir. They want us to move."

I had been asleep stretched out on the front seat and was now struggling to sit up and slip my legs out of the sleeping bag. Sadly, the gear lever and the steering wheel ganged up against me and I tumbled out of the bus like clothes bag from a laundry chute. My new worm's eye perspective showed me a shining steel blade hovering above me with James' upside-down face in the background and behind him, also upside down, the face of a man wearing a military beret.

"Good evening, sir," said the face under the beret. By now he was the right way up and so was I. "Who are you, sir and what are doing here?"

"Well," I said stiffly. "We are peaceful British travellers and we are camping for the night. There are six of us."

"But what are you doing *here?* In this dangerous place?" The soldier was a handsome, young officer with keen, intelligent eyes. His English was almost

'Home Counties' quality but his tone was censorious and curt. Beyond him, down on the road, were two big army lorries full of troops.

"We're on our way to Quetta."

"Quetta?" He exclaimed, staring unbelievingly. "We took a wrong turning some miles back and —"

"I see. Well, I cannot permit you to stay here. You must continue your journey."

"What now! At…er…four in the morning?"

"Now, whatever time it is."

"But all my companions are asleep. It isn't easy to strike camp in the dark. Look, what…"

"No sir," he said firmly, shaking his head. "Here it is unsafe. We will give you what help we can. Please be quick. We will be escort for you to a safe place and then you will travel to Quetta without problems."

He shouted some instructions and half a dozen men jumped down from the second truck.

I let my breath go loudly out of annoyance, but I couldn't blame the fellow. After all, his views had simply confirmed my own feeling about the spot. But what a pest – I had been enjoying such a lovely and much needed sleep!

"Wake everyone up James. And tell them to hurry. We are setting off right away."

The young officer picked up the machete which James had dropped and courteously handed it to me, handle first.

"Hardly a match, sir," he said drily, "for what your neighbours might use. It may interest you to know, sir, that attacks on our units are often happening in this region and we have had many casualties. You are fortunate we come this way and find you."

"Believe me, Lieutenant, I understand all you say and am grateful. I think that within five or six minutes we shall be ready to move."

It was in fact more like ten or twelve. Already pretty shattered by what they'd endured over days of tough travelling, interrupted sleep was now another burden my young adventurers had to tackle. Feeling some sympathy, I forbore hectoring or chivvying them to get a move on and let the process of striking camp and loading up run on autopilot. The Pakistan army would just have to be patient!

Placing ourselves, as directed, astern the first army lorry and ahead of the second, I felt dragooned rather than escorted. Despite some moonlight, little or nothing of the surrounding terrain could be glimpsed and at first all I could see was a billowing cloud of thick dust though which the taillights of the lead truck fuzzily glimmered. It was a tough drive but once I had got the second lorry to accept that I was not prepared to ride the bumper of the first, I was able to see the road surface in my own lights and so protect the bus from the worst of the potholes and stray rocks.

Daylight saw us a couple of thousand feet above the village of Qilla Abdullah with the road ahead zigzagging down to it in serpentine splendour. Our little convoy had halted and its soldiers were jumping down to stretch their legs.

"We shall leave you here" said the young lieutenant marching up to my window, looking surprisingly fresh and awake. "Down there this road meets the highway going from the Khojak Pass to Quetta." he added, pointing down towards Qilla Abdullah. He peered into the back of the bus and I turned round to share his view. It was a world of twisted and contorted limbs, tousled hair and bemused hard-to-keep-open eyes.

"They'll be fine after a bite to eat."

"And a wash!" We exchanged smiles. "Thank you, lieutenant, for your help."

"Our duty. The road down, by the way, is very steep. You have good brakes?"

"Should be OK. But thanks for the warning." He saluted and I started up, steering round and squeezing past the big lorry to the cheerful waves of Pakistan's finest.

Chapter 19

We reached Quetta just after eleven and went straight to the railway station, learning that the train from Nok Kundi had arrived about seven the previous evening. And, yes, a helpful railway official cheerfully confirmed he had seen some English boys get off the train and exit the station. Unfortunately, neither he nor anyone else had any idea where they had gone thereafter.

"What now, sir?" asked Jason Wright.

"Nothing to it, Jason, my friend," I replied in a blandly serious voice. "Only half a million people live in Quetta, so we're bound to come across them sooner or later!"

"Yes sir. I suppose…"

Leaving his sentence unfinished, Jason's expression exuded a wonderful mix of serious doubt and loyal acceptance. He then turned to see what had suddenly grabbed my attention. His sudden smile was gorgeous.

"Hi! So, you've made it at last."

"Roy! By all that's wonderful! How did you know we'd arrived? I've just been telling Jason here it would be easy to find you, but he somehow doubted my assurance."

"One of us has been coming to the station to check more or less every hour."

"Fantastic!"

"Where are the rest of your gang?"

"At the hotel. We booked in last night. The Imdad Hotel. A bit grotty of course, but pretty good all told. It's in Jinnah Road – the main street. Just opposite."

"Great. And the trailer?"

"All taken care of. New tyres fitted last night and then we pushed it round to the hotel."

"Roy! How do you do it? But come on, take us to this famous hotel of yours. A nice wash and —"

"They even do cold beer, but it has to be in your room."

"Roy, what can I say? Of course, any fool can book a hotel, but it takes real genius to hire a slice of paradise."

"I suppose you will have heard the news about India," said Roy as we sat down to enjoy the promised cold beer on the balcony outside our room. About two hours had elapsed since our reunion and in that time, I had showered, changed and managed a bite of lunch.

"Since leaving Nok Kundi, Roy, we've been out of touch with the twentieth century. I've heard not a breath of news, about India or anywhere else."

"Wow...Well then, hang on to your seat. It doesn't sound good to me. Quite worrying, really. You remember the bother India was having last June, just before we set off in fact, with some Sikh militants who'd locked themselves inside their Golden Temple in Amritsar?"

"Yes, I do. In fact..."

"Well Mrs Gandhi is now accusing Pakistan of supporting these Sikh rebels and has retaliated by closing the frontier."

This news was as serious as it was, to me, unexpected. In June, Indira Gandhi had ordered the Indian Army to break into the Sikh's most holy shrine – where it was sacrilege for any but Sikhs to enter – to expel armed Sikh rebels who were demanding self-rule and effect the establishment of an independent Sikh state. At the time this news had broken upon the world I had contacted the Indian High Commission in London to ask if these Sikh troubles might make it unsafe or impractical to travel through the Punjab in general and through the city of Amritsar in particular. The Indian reply had been exceedingly robust, essentially telling me that these Sikh troubles were nothing more than a 'little local difficulty' and that by the time we arrived in Amritsar in August the whole business would be 'over and forgotten'.

Obviously, judging from Roy's statement, the Indian High Commission's view had been hopelessly optimistic and we now had a very serious and entirely unexpected difficulty facing us. The key to understanding the gravity of our situation is to appreciate that the one thousand five hundred miles long land frontier between India and Pakistan was and still is, totally and wholly unlike any European frontier such as, for example, between Norway and Sweden or France and Spain. The India-Pakistan frontier, in basic terms, is a military truce demarcation line between two countries who had made war upon one another more than once in the recent past and who still shared much suspicion of one another and harboured little mutual good will. The second essential point to grasp is that this long, long frontier had only one, single, usable, authorised crossing point and that was at Amritsar.

To add to our worries, every alternative to our existing plan carried serious and probably insurmountable difficulties. I spelt these out as Roy as I discussed our options.

"For a start, Roy, I have to say that the first obvious thought, namely, to return home the way we have come, is almost certainly impracticable. To begin with, our existing Iranian transit visas which, let's face it, were obtained by a bloody miracle, are one-way only and the chances of getting another set out here in Pakistan, I would guess are close to nil. Besides, it's now mid-August and the new school year, as you know all too well, is due to begin early in September. Three weeks is hardly time enough to drive all the way back to the UK along a route that we know from our own painful experience takes a minimum of six if you're lucky. And I can just picture in my mind's eye the thoughts of the School Trustees as their headmaster waltzes on to the premises three weeks late. And with not a single act of preparation carried out. No timetable, no form lists, no nothing!"

"So, are you suggesting we sort of abandon ship and fly back from, say, Karachi?"

"It would be a nice relief in one sense, but it isn't practical politics. Not to re- export the bus would cost the school a fortune and don't forget all those airline tickets already bought which relate to a flight from Delhi."

"So…what are you saying? Surely…"

"What I am saying is let's not panic. It is quite possible that by the time we get to Amritsar the border will have been reopened. After all it must be damaging to India to cut itself off from trading with its neighbour."

Roy raised his eyebrows in an elegant statement of unspoken doubt.

"So" I added, the historian in me surfacing, "like the Duke of Medina Sidonia, the commander of Philip II's Armada, we shall have 'to travel onward in the confident expectation of a miracle'."

Quetta itself was in festive mood, still winding down from the celebrations held two days earlier marking August 14th, Pakistan's National Day. Green and white flags fluttered everywhere and poster portraits of the President, General Zia-ul-Haq, had been used to tart-up virtually every wall in sight. The bustling thoroughfares and buzzing bazars were thronged with fierce-looking bearded Pathans, so obvious in their distinctive clothes and long-striding, lissom movements. Today's Pathans are heirs to a long and strange tradition of giving Tommy Atkins, according to time and circumstance, either devoted service or implacable enmity. Luckily for our guys, Atkins' schoolboy brothers of Orwell's Year, those we met were friendly and good natured to a man.

Architecturally Quetta is a comparatively new and lacklustre place, a catastrophic earthquake in 1935 having almost entirely destroyed the old Moghul city, but it is neat and well kept. In the area around the railway station, it is easy to imagine yourself back in the great days of British India. 'Quetta Station' and the 'Post and Telegraph Office' have bold, English-only signage to proclaim their functions and stand serene, if slightly shabby; homely and dignified in their Anglo-Moghul architecture. The Governor's House still looks like a large Edwardian vicarage. About two thirds of Quetta is taken up by the Military Cantonment, laid out when the city was a vital frontier post of Imperial India and is still today an important centre for the Pakistan Army, whose main Staff College is here. The whole place has strong echoes of Aldershot: Its 'lines' 18 laid out with geometric precision, its garrison church and its many garden-girt bungalows clearly English in pedigree. Whilst in Quetta we made time for a brief tour of the cantonment area, visiting the bungalow once used by field Marshall.

Montgomery when he was a mere major. It now houses a fascinating museum of army life in British India.

There are two main routes from Quetta to the colourful and dynamic city of Lahore, for centuries the capital of the Punjab and now the one and only stepping off point for entry into Hindu India from fiercely Muslim Pakistan. The shorter route, more northerly and passing through Ziarat, Loralai and Fort Munro, was said to be superb as to scenery but risky to use; even the official Pakistan Tourist Ministry recommending intending travellers to arrange for an escort. This route was also reported as rough and largely unsurfaced and this, with the troubles of our trailer fresh in mind, perhaps more than anything made us decide upon the longer alternative via the Bolan Pass.

The Bolan, intimidating and majestic in all its rocky heights and umbral chasms, offered us unforgettable cameos of Pakistan's rural life. The sixty-mile Bolan Pass, used by countless invaders over several millennia to pass from central Asia down into the Indian subcontinent, is said by many to be more awe-inspiring even than the better-known Khyber. In 1841, during the First Afghan War, an entire British detachment was drowned in the Bolan in a flash flood. Essentially the pass carries both road and rail through a series of stupendous narrow gorges until they have descended some five thousand or more feet to the plains.

Growling and labouring buses and lorries, making their way at walking pace up the steeper sections, are among the more fascinating aspects of the Bolan. Grossly overloaded and, as often as not belching clouds of black diesel, these vehicles must be the most gaudy and ornate on the planet. Not a square inch of bodywork escapes the rash of decoration. Beautifully painted arabesque designs and floral scrollwork predominate, but full-blown pictures of mosques or landscapes are also favoured. All this, of course, simply serves to establish a basic theme and is an underlay upon which galactic quantities of glass beads and bright pearly ornamentation is superimposed. No sequin-drenched ballroom gown would come near to rivalling the sheeny excrescences trowelled onto a Bolan bus. Fringes and tassels, streamers and banners also hang from every conceivable anchorage. The inside of the bus is, needless to say, subjected to a similar decorative maelstrom.

Prompted by successive motorcades of overloaded buses and trucks, I suggested pairs of boys, taking turns, might like to ride on our rooftop luggage rack, a licence enthusiastically taken up. Our new top deck accommodation was great for camerawork as well as a marvellous platform for trading greetings – and insults – with the numerous outriding passengers of many of the buses and trucks.

As well as serving modern motor traffic, the Bolan continues its age-old role as conduit for nomadic peoples moving between the hills and the plains with their dromedaries and donkeys and their flocks of fat-tailed sheep. At our stopping places, where we snacked and stretched our limbs, we watched these trains glide by as though pageants of Old Testament scenes were being staged for our benefit. First came the veiled women walking past in the dust with pitchers on their heads, leading little children by the hand. Then, at times, an aloof and mysterious sister or respected matriarch would follow, cosseted atop a dromedary and hidden within a swaying tent of diaphanous cottons. There were sturdy shepherd-boys too, with croaky voices worn out from urging on their thin and thirsty beasts. Friendly lads as a rule and ever ready to return our smiles and waves. Young men also passed, often driving donkeys prodigiously loaded, these fellows fierce of face and gaunt and occasionally proudly disdainful. At intervals small knots of long-bearded, turbaned patriarchs also came along, controlling and separating the other elements like punctuation in a sentence, their long walking staffs ringing out on the road against their silent, easy strides.

In the lower reaches of the pass, the Bolan River became alive again, at first no more than a tumbling stream splashing over pebble and boulder but later a proper river, brown and smooth-flowing. Every meal stops then became a swimming stop where bridges and roadside prominences served as diving boards for the daring. Still further down reedy banks appeared where water buffaloes grazed and sometimes swam with small boys hitched upon their backs. Phil Cairns, reluctant to accept that such a pastime was beyond the compass of an English boy, swam out and signalled that he would like to come aboard. The naked jockey, wide-eyed but happy, made room but the beast, objecting to the extra weight, or perhaps an alien odour, engineered a gentle capsize to the hysterical delight of the spectators, local and English alike.

For all our gnawing anxieties about the troubled Indo-Pakistan situation and its effect on our future, this period was the Indian summer of our journey: Unhurried, relaxing days providing a hundred and one delights.

Chapter 20

Lahore, one of the great Moghul cities of old India, ranks with Delhi or Agra in its range of superb Muslim architecture. Its busy streets and bazaars cry out for exploration and its mix of both Islamic and British architecture ensures it is a city of surprises and charming contrasts. 'Queen of the Punjab' for a thousand years, even the cruel blow of Partition in 1947 has done little to diminish its importance. It is Pakistan's second city.

Our run into Lahore coincided with the torrential rains and flooded streets of the monsoon, making any notion of camping a non-starter. Although it was but ten paces from our parked vehicle to the modest portals of the Al-Noor Hotel, the downpour was such that we burst into its lobby resembling drowned rats. Sadly, almost criminally, the price of our rather leisured progress down from Quetta was that our time in Lahore had to be brief and it was therefore impossible to experience more than a sample of what the city offered. As a party of schoolboys, surely, we were right to make Zamzama or Kim's Gun our first priority. It still stands, as in Kipling's day, in front of the Central Museum, but nowadays the spot is a lake-surrounded island in the middle of a busy road and the ambition of Phil Cairns to sit astride the gun and once again claim the Punjab for the British had to be abandoned. The Central Museum, built by the British in their usual flamboyant Moghul Gothic and acknowledged to be the best museum in Pakistan, was our second objective. Its first curator, by the way, was Rudyard Kipling's father. The glories of the Badshahi Mosque also claimed our attention and I imagine few would dispute its status as one of the world's most beautiful Islamic buildings. It is, I believe, the largest mosque ever built before modern times and is said to have room for sixty thousand worshipers.

Before we entered the mosque, we of course removed our shoes, leaving them in a neat line in the charge of a small and very cheerful minder aged, I would guess, eight or nine. When we returned an hour or so later, we found the little fellow in a state of great distress. His English was very rudimentary, but it appeared that 'a very important man' had come, removed his own shoes and then, ignoring the boy's protests, had put on

148

Alan Beattie's almost new and very superior, trainers and marched off. The strangest thing of all was that the mysterious shoe bandit had left behind a pretty decent pair of Oxford brogues; shoes only likely to be worn in Pakistan by a person of education and high social standing! Alan, of course was furious and absolutely refused to consider taking the brogues in exchange. Tactlessly forgetting that brogues were a shoe that I sometimes wore, he made it crystal clear that he would not be seen dead wearing such a naff article! The Great Oriental Shoe Mystery remains unsolved to this very day. To add a final touch of irony, so as to cheer up the distraught shoe-guardian I upped his promised fee by a factor of ten.

"In rewarding failure, headmaster," teased Roy, "you've probably set the child in the direction of a life of crime."

"Could be," I responded, pointing over my shoulder towards the shoe racks. "But if you really feel that way, try getting our money back from him."

By then the child was surrounded by a mob of other urchins, all chattering excitedly. News travels fast in the Orient.

Midway through the afternoon of Tuesday August 21st we arrived at Wagah, the actual town at the border with India. There were long lines of buses and trucks parked either side of the main street, many with their crews resting in the shade under them. Knots of listless people stood about doing nothing in particular and nobody appeared to mind as I drove slowly to the front of the queue and pulled up outside the Pakistan Passport Control building.

"Is it possible to pass over to India?" I asked the first senior looking official I met.

"What passports do you have?"

"British."

"And visas for India and health certificates?" I nodded.

"I don't know. I think they are closed for everyone." He shrugged. "Maybe it will be OK for British."

"How can I find out?"

"You must walk, it's maybe four or five hundred metres, to the Indian control at the other side. I will give you a paper so you can pass our military. If the Indians say 'yes', then you come back and we will do exit procedures."

But the Indians said 'no'. Very firmly indeed.

I have rarely been so sick at heart or as worried or as uncertain about what to do next as in the minutes following the Indian Authorities point blank refusal to let us into the country. Plan A for delivering one-off minibus to Lepra had come unstuck and I had no plan B. Of course, in an ideal world there should have been but I had used up all my available time and resources in cobbling together our basic scheme for delivering our gift to Lepra and in the end it had boiled down to one simple, straight question: Did we go for it, or did we not? And we had gone!

On my return everyone guessed at once from my round-shouldered hangdog pathos that my mission had not been successful. It had not been for want of trying and at every stage of my negotiations I had stressed the youthful vulnerability and urgent needs of my passengers and had vigorously challenged the statements and pronouncements of the Indian officials. I had been difficult and demanded access to ever more senior officials. In the end, after a lot of argy-bargy and a two hour wait, I had even managed to get an interview with the commander himself of this strategically important border post; in itself quite an achievement. He had been courteous and gracious but equally brisk and to the point. His government had ordered the frontier with Pakistan to be closed and that was that.

"We learned from your people many, many years ago," he finished, looking at me archly over the top of his gold-rimmed glasses, "that 'orders are orders' is the only way to run an army, or indeed any government department." And no, he would not telegraph a request to Delhi for a special exception to be made because it would do no good. The Sikh unrest in the Punjab was serious and the frontier was likely to remain closed for some time.

"It is no good trying to cross anywhere else, Adrian," I explained, answering one of a dozen speculative and anxious questions. "This is the *one and only* land crossing point of the entire frontier between India and Pakistan."

"And going back the way we came?"

"We've been through it all before," I answered wearily. "You are talking about four or five weeks of travel at the very least and that is after getting down to Karachi and after getting Iranian visas."

"If they decide to grant them," added Roy.

"Quiet! And you all know how touch and go it was getting them in London, to say the least of it."

"We are probably on the Ayatollah's death list by now anyway," said Phil Cairns in doleful tones.

All this was being said as we were holding a crisis meeting whilst sitting on the ground in a circle by the bus. Around us, looking on in fascination and with oriental insensibility to any notion of invaded privacy, stood a second circle of locals, themselves doubtless victims of the closed frontier. We must have made a sorry and dispirited spectacle. I, for one, feeling like a Saxon on the day after Hastings.

"Come on," I sighed wearily, as I sensed the weighty mantle of leadership around my sagging shoulders. "Let's pack up and get going. It's about a thousand miles to Karachi and it won't get any nearer by sitting here."

Chapter 21

It was dark by the time we had made it back through Lahore and had gained the main road south to Multan. Given the endless heavy rain which we were now suffering we chose to travel on through the early part of the night as trying to set up camp in the dark and the downpour would have been ridiculous. Besides, it somehow suited my mood to press on, measuring up to the demands of the driving giving me a strange sense of sour satisfaction.

Night driving on Pakistan's main highways, at any rate back in the 1980s, was a very dangerous business. For a start the roads were only just wide enough for two trucks to pass one another, quite literally, a hand's breadth apart. In the monsoon period in particular, where the cracked and crumbling tarmac ends a quagmire begins and a wheel off the tarmac easily becomes a plunge down an embankment and a catastrophic rollover. Few trucks had a full set of working lights and it was not uncommon to come across a specimen without any taillights at all or, say, with only one headlamp working and that, probably on high beam and ill-set. Yet these were minor hazards when set against the many bullock carts plodding along without any lights at all. When all is said and done, though, even a loaded bullock cart presents a slight elasticity when impacted; something which cannot be said of massive broken-down trucks, unlit and abandoned just wherever they happened to have conked out.

For all the overloaded state and dubious mechanical condition of their vehicles, a compulsive urge to overtake one another seemed endemic amongst Pakistan's bus and truck drivers, their antics making Russian roulette appear no more than the stuff of kindergartens. In this gung-ho world of Muslim fatalism, a minibus draws a short straw. On the one hand it lacks a car's acceleration and manoeuvrability, whilst on the other, despite its size, it is still a bantam in any scrummage of trucks and buses.

Next morning, luckily at low speed, the trailer tow bar sheared off the bus and we had to make a rope and wire lash-up until, a few miles later, we came to a village with a welder. Third World welders are far more ambitious than their counterparts in technically advanced nations and over the years I have had all sorts of failed components magically welded at some very out of the way places. Snapped off half- shafts, missing gear teeth and a badly cracked chassis all come to mind with a sense of wonder and gratitude as instances of successful repairs that would never have been contemplated in lands where white coats and well-equipped workshops are commonplace. Even so, in my view the fearless welder of the Punjabi village of Piran Ghaib caps the lot of them.

The broken tow bar had been anchored to a substantial chassis cross member via a thick bracket and it was in this bracket where the fracture had occurred. This same chassis member also part-supported the petrol tank. Finding it impossible to free four rusted bolts required to come out for complete disassembly, our audacious rural technician announced he would affect the repair by re-welding the anchor bracket where it was. *'Never teach your grandmother to suck eggs'* is an aphorism to which, as a rule, I heartily subscribe but, in this instance, I felt it would not be entirely insensitive to draw the fellow's attention to the close proximity of sixty litres of petrol half an inch beyond his intended scene of operation. To drain the tank of petrol and refill it temporarily with water, I realised, would be a frightful time-consuming bore but what alternative was there?

Having sufficient faith in the Almighty was, of course, the answer. Lying on his back on the sand behind his face-shield, in reply the old boy pointed a finger heavenwards and shrugged – a gesture I took to mean he felt it was all in Allah's hands. Doubtless the same philosophy was shared by his two ten-year-old assistants who, armed with blue-tinted goggles and a small tin of water apiece, lay on their stomachs beside their boss beneath our bus. Whilst I should hate to be labelled a 'man of little faith', I confess that in the circumstances I felt it incumbent upon me to order out of the bus the boys resting there and then to insist all my party should retire at least twenty yards from the vehicle.

After much yanking of a starting handle by a third Punjabi youth, an engine started and lights came on in the nearby workshop. More to the point, a great and continuous shower of sparks then issued from beneath the bus, accompanied from time to time by a fair amount of hammering. At length the two mini-mechanics and the intrepid welder wriggled out from under the bus, the latter at the same time pronouncing our troubles over.

"She ees fixed," translated one of the small boys, a big friendly grin splitting his oily face.

Just in case the matter is misunderstood, I must make it clear that the cans of water which accompanied the two Pakistani boys in their duties had nothing whatever to do with dousing flames should Allah not have been minded to protect His own from the combustibility of petrol. There could not have been any help at all on that score had things gone wrong! No, the water they had was to suppress such welding sparks as alighted on their employer, a wisp of smoke rising from his beard and a distinct smell of singed hair giving testament to the importance of their role.

Sind, the southernmost province of Pakistan stretches northward from the Arabian Sea on either side of the Indus, bounded in the west by the deserts of Baluchistan and in the east by the Thar desert of India. Sind has historical roots rivalling those of Egypt and Mesopotamia and has cities dating back over five thousand years. These civilisations bordering the Indus, like those of Egypt, were hugely dependent upon seasonal river flooding to maintain the fertility of the land and this precarious reliance on a destructive but life-giving force governed every aspect of life in the region. That is, until 1932 when the British Administration built the mighty Sukkur Barrage, taming the River Indus and creating out of the desert wastes some thirty-three million acres of fertile land. A whole province-full of farmland conjured out of a desert wilderness!

When we reached Sukkur around midday on Thursday, August 23rd, morale within our company was at its very lowest level. All through the previous night the monsoon rain had been incessant, making our overnight stop a misery and easily the worst we had so far experienced. Our bodies had provided a binge feast for a million mosquitoes whereas heat and humidity had made much of our own food inedible. Boys often found on opening their bags that supposedly clean clothing was tinged with green mould. Indeed, such was the climatic torment that every aspect of existence might just as well have been carried out within a Turkish bath. Arguments and disputes would arise out of nothing and long, stony faces stared unseeing and uninterested at the passing landscape. Our expedition had plainly lost its momentum and was beginning to fall apart largely thanks to my poor leadership over these last two days where I had allowed my frustrations, disappointment and worries to monopolise my thoughts.

The road south crosses the Indus on the actual Sukkur barrage, the whole scene being highly impressive as millions of tons of boiling brown water pound their way through the sluices. Both as an engineering marvel and as a triumph of

Man over Nature, the Sukkur Barrage commands attention, yet the boys showed as much interest as if I had pointed to a dead dog at the roadside.

Just beyond the barrage I caught sight of a large modern building perched high above the road. It stood out like a sore thumb, alien to its surroundings and deliberately so. As we came closer, I saw it was a luxury hotel, a huge electric sign on its flat roof proclaiming it to be the *'Interpak Inn'*. A long winding drive, lined with posh looking streetlamps connected it to the road we were on and, on a spur of the moment decision I suddenly swerved into the drive to lurch to a stop a few minutes later in front of the hotel. My unexpected and pretty violent manoeuvre had at least wiped ten please-feel-sorry-for-me expressions from ten youthful faces. The new universal mask was of the what-the-hell-is-going-on category: Perhaps progress of a sort!

"Sir, what have we stopped for?" Whined someone from behind.

"Roy," I said, ignoring the question, "let us spend a couple of minutes in the hotel.

"All of us?" asked Adrian.

"No. You will please all stay in the bus. We shan't be long."

"But sir, it's sweltering here. Can't we —"

"No. Pakistan happens to be a hot country, laddie, so you'll just have to lump it."

"OK Mr Beckford?"

Roy affirmed he was, but I could see he was taken aback by my trenchant and unfeeling dismissal of Adrian's request.

"Sorry to take you by surprise, Roy, but I'm fed up with the negative misery we are all wallowing in. The expedition is falling apart, everyone is bickering and I just can't let it go on."

"I agree. Of course, the main trouble…"

"Oh, I know we've suffered a huge setback and terrific disappointment, but so what? This is an adventure and uncertainty is part of adventure. If everything was always going to run like clockwork and be wholly predictable, it would hardly be an adventure. *We…I…*gambled on the frontier being open. OK, I was wrong but hang it all even getting this far is bloody good for a school trip in an old minibus."

There was a good deal more in the same vein and, to tell the truth, much of what I said was to buck up my own morale as much as anyone else's.

"Listen, Roy," I went on. "The lads are fine at heart. They just need cheering up. Boys are like dogs. No matter what's gone wrong, give them a good feed and they'll be fine. Napoleon said as much. Here they are marching along with nothing but heat, rain and mosquitoes. If it's not mud at every turn, then it's dust and desiccation. And, worse, nothing but stale old camp muck to eat at the end of it. When I spotted this place, I suddenly thought: *The rich in Pakistan, they won't grub about in muddy camps when they travel. For them it'll be nothing but the best. Air-conditioning, showers, proper toilets, fine food.* My idea, Roy, is to give the troops a slap-up meal, a chance for a good wash. Perhaps a swim. There'll be a pool in a hotel like this. You can bet your life on it."

"It'll cost a bomb."

"I know, I know. But I also know if we do this we'll get back on an even keel. I haven't a clue what is going to happen or how we are going to get ourselves back home. But I've been in some tight spots before and I'm not beaten yet. True, I have been really worried these last few days but that's because I've allowed myself to dwell on the negative. Anyway, to hell with the damned Indians and Iranians and their tin pot regimes. We're going to get back somehow. That's for sure."

"Even if we have to walk!" said Roy, smiling wryly.

"Come on, let's ask about prices and hear the worst. That guy at the reception desk is giving us funny looks."

We had been talking in the palatial entrance lounge, a lofty cathedral-like place of striking elegance, dotted with fountains and palms. Much of the floor space was given over to intimate clusters of leather sofas, oversized armchairs and elaborately embossed bronze-topped coffee tables, each grouping being at a different level and linked to the whole by steps and low walls stylishly executed in polished marble that matched the floor. White-gloved stewards glided about attending to groups of smartly dressed guests.

By the time Roy had properly parked up the bus and had then chivvied the boys into changing into their cleanest clothes I had booked lunch and negotiated the loan of a bedroom so that we could all take a shower. Having first managed a modest clean-up of my own, I was down just in time to meet Roy and the gang as, ocean-eyed with disbelief and wonder, they entered a rare world where the steamy filth of the monsoon had no place.

"Sit over there," I ordered, pointing to a fortress of sofas and chairs where menu cards had been laid out. "And" I added, deliberately using my most schoolmasterly voice, for I was still cross with them all, "think carefully about your choices because I don't want any annoying mind changes or similar silly nonsenses." As we all sat poring over the menu, I despatched pairs of boys turn by turn to our hired bedroom with orders to make themselves fit to re-join civilisation and not dare to leave the marble and gold tapped en-suite facility other than as they found it. They did well, bless them and by the time the last pair had returned I was again happy to be in their company and feeling a good deal less grumpy.

Leaving them all prattling away happily, most seemingly engaged in defending or promoting their individual menu choices, I wandered over to the entrance where a sizeable group of newcomers had arrived. Important folk too, if the number and attentiveness of the hotel porters was anything to go by.

"Velcome to Pakistan, sir. How many games will you be having? It is not often these days that we see an English school cricket team in our country and I was wondering if you happen to have played against my old school in Lahore. Have you had success in your tour?"

A little earlier I had noticed a distinguished looking and very smartly dressed fellow sitting on his own in the lounge, seemingly fascinated by our presence and our doings. Now this same man was standing beside me. His eyes danced with amusement at my surprise. Clearly, I had to put him right as to our credentials and the purpose of our presence in Pakistan, but this only had the effect of increasing his interest in us.

"My, my! What an adventure!" He had exclaimed after I had outlined our journey and its raison d'etre. "But I'm not surprised you are in trouble. India is always difficult and touchy and Iran is at war with itself as much as with Iraq. At the moment, then, you are travelling to Karachi?"

"Yes, I think our only realistic option is to see if the British Consul will help us get flights back to England and advise how we can somehow ship the bus back. We are legally obliged to do that. I suppose it might theoretically be possible to return the way we came but I am very unsure about getting Iranian visas and, anyway, it will take too long. School starts early in September."

The school cricket enthusiast glanced at his watch and rubbed his chin thoughtfully.

"Look," he said. "I am a government minister and I think I can be of some help to you. But right now, I have a meeting with all these delegates who have just arrived. Can you wait an hour or so? I have friends and contacts in Karachi and will be able to telephone people."

I had hardly begun to splutter my thanks when he held up his hand. "Sorry, I must go. I'll see you in one hour or a little more."

If there is a male equivalent of a fairy godmother, my new acquaintance was he. Quite simply from that precise moment our luck dramatically, radically and almost unbelievably changed. Never at any point in my life have I experienced such a rapid and abrupt change in fortune. For some time I stood stock still where I was, fearing that if I re-joined Roy and the boys to put them in the picture my voice would disintegrate from welled-up emotion.

After our splendid lunch, during which I managed to give Roy no more than a hint that our fortunes might have passed their nadir, we reoccupied the sofas and armchairs of our old redoubt to await the promised return of Mr Nasir Khan, as the minister was called. Pretty well on cue the hubbub of men in suits drifted back into the great lounge, the minister among them, most making their way to the exit but a few taking seats and ordering refreshment. A little later, having shed the last of his garrulous companions, Mr Khan strode over to us and pushed a scrap of paper into my hand.

"I have just tried to speak to a friend of mine on the telephone, Jimmy Katrak. He is in shipping and I deal with civil aviation so we meet quite often. I've put his address on that paper. He's not at home at the moment but I've spoken to his son and explained your problem. He will tell his father about it. Jimmy will help you and fix everything. That paper has his business address and telephone and his home address. When you reach Karachi you must telephone to him. He will ship your bus on the first available vessel and Pakistan International will fly you and your boys to Bombay where you will be able to resume your wonderful journey. The air tickets will be complimentary but I can't say about the ship."

Hardly giving me chance to even begin to express my thanks, Mr Khan went on:

"I now fly to Islamabad so I must leave you. I have ordered cakes and cola for your boys, so happy returns." Brushing aside all my attempts to thank him, he then shook hands with Roy and I and with each boy before rushing off, only pausing to say: "Jimmy Katrak is very experienced and a very good man. Trust him totally". And with that he was gone.

"Well," said a dropped jaw Roy, after I had explained what lay behind the minister's words, "they say that the age of miracles has passed. How bloody wrong they are!"

Chapter 22

Which sees us recommence our journey to Karachi in a new mood of buoyant optimism. We also find time to play international cricket before arriving at the offices of Katrak & Company.

"It's remarkable, isn't it?" philosophised Roy from the driving seat as we made what distance we could before nightfall, "that no matter how backward or chaotic the place, the moment you breeze into a spot the rich use, everything works. Look how easy it was for Mr Khan to telephone his friends in Karachi. I bet it would have been a different story if he had tried to phone from somewhere in the back streets of Sukkur."

"You have a point Roy but as a geographer do you have a theory to account for it?"

"It's called *gravy.*"

"Sir," called out Adrian from behind. "May I ask how much the lunch cost?"

"Roughly thirty dollars a head."

"Which," chipped in Roy, "is about what the average Pakistani earns in a year." Roy's comment sparked off quite a noisy debate.

"Sir, what do you think the waiters and people feel?" asked James. "I mean they must think it disgusting that you spent so much dosh on kids like us?"

"Speak for yourself, James" retorted Phil, sensing an opening for mischief. "They probably steal like mad," said Slackie. "I would in their place."

"We know that but thankfully not everyone is like you," countered Phil. "Well, if the system is rotten what else can you do?" Demanded Slackie. "Not everyone has a filthy rich lawyer as his daddy, or is that news to you?"

And so, the debate rattled on – a mix of the serious and the abusive as is often the way with schoolboys. But it was good to hear many of them making mature and perceptive points, illustrating the shift from the *'me, me'* of the child to using their imaginations to see things from the perspective of others. Equally, it was rewarding to note in some of them a questioning of the social assumptions inherent in their own backgrounds.

Next day as we approached the important city of Hyderabad the landscape became greener and villages began to appear thick and fast. Lines of camels, all burdened by enormous loads of farm produce, became a common sight; each beast perfectly positioned in the camel crocodile and each plodding along the edge of the road with the same dignified jerky gait and wearing the same sardonic expression. Files of women, all with pitchers or baskets elegantly balanced on their heads, displaying heights of natural grace that no backpack carrying European can hope to equal, also claimed their share of the highway. They were all totally unfazed by passing trucks slicing by just inches from them. And clumps of water buffalo were also users of the road, placidly sauntering along in lazy comfort, as immune to the shrill urging of their pint-sized barefoot minders as they were to the raucous horn blowing of impatient trucks.

A pleasing sight in many of the villages passed through was that of youngsters playing cricket in all manner of quaint or improvised circumstances.

"We should stop and give the locals a game," suggested Craig, contributing to a desultory discussion on the general strength of Pakistan in international cricket which at that point happened to be the topic in the everchanging kaleidoscope of passenger conversation.

"Well, we do happen to have a bat and ball with us somewhere," said Roy. "I remember packing them. On the roof I think."

Both Roy and Craig were keen and capable cricketers. With yet another village coming up, our road was now running on a curved embankment which happened to circle a dried-up lake where some cricket was taking place.

"Here's your chance," I called over my shoulder, applying the brakes and pulling *over* off the carriageway. Warning all to take care with the traffic, I suggested to Craig that he ran down the embankment to ask if he could join in the game.

It was hardly Lord's. The basic surface was crazed and hardened mud, smoothed over to some extent on the actual wicket. A battered oil drum served as the stumps and the bowler's end was marked by a planted stick. At the moment of our arrival both the bowling and batting were being monopolised by older teenagers whereas the fielders were small boys of, I guess, ten or twelve. The bat in use was but a crudely shaped length of plank and the ball a well-worn make-do from tennis. I suspect the import of Craig's cheery 'mind if we join in?' Escaped the local players but the bat and ball he held aloft were enough to proclaim his general intent. At all events the hospitality of the home side was both instantaneous and impeccable, they somehow divining that for them to bat and for us to field would suit both parties.

Craig, wisely surmising that our *'Jack Hatfield Signed Special'* would confer an advantage, sportingly lent our bat to Pakistan's twelve-year-old opener. The lad was so awestruck – presumably his first handling of a proper bat – that the novelty of the experience seemed almost to overwhelm him. Several minutes were then taken up in his showing the hallowed item to his pals, our 'internationals' meanwhile using the delay to arrange their field. Just as play at last was about to begin, a small dispute between Roy, in his role as umpire and Craig occurred. Craig, as opening bowler, had had it in mind to use our brand new, shiny and pukka, red leather ball but Roy, fearing players unused to a hard ball might be injured, insisted the local team's-tired tennis ball be used, despite Craig's protest that it was 'vile and slimy'.

Mr Nasir Khan's initial assumption that our party must be a touring cricket team was wrong, as it were, twice over. First, obviously in that our purpose all along had been to deliver a bus to 'Lepra' in India; but second, because only Craig Bradley, Alan Beattie and David Armstrong could by any stretch of the imagination be described as cricketers at all. The rest, who by chance happened to be amongst those opting during the summer term to do either rowing or athletics, were, broadly speaking, rabbits as far as cricket was concerned. This showed particularly in the fielding where several easy catches were shamefully botched. Nonetheless Craig and David bowled with creditable effectiveness, particularly given the unusual nature of the pitch and before too long fourteen of Pakistan's batsmen had been dismissed. This, I have to say, was despite Umpire Roy's astonishing rejection of several howzat backed up by resounding clangs as the ball thumped against the oil drum. The home side also supplied a young scorer complete with notebook and pencil. Unfortunately, his tally was impossible for our side to decipher, it being set down in beautiful right-to-left Urdu script. Pakistan declared once all its young batsmen were out, the three or four older ones who had not yet batted, I imagine, wanting to save their energies for bowling.

By now there was a sizeable crowd of spectators on the boundary – which was where the baked mud of the field gave way to grass. Most of the village must have been there. There were even quite a few women watching, clustered together on the far side of the road in feminine isolation and very distinctive in their *kameezes* and colourful baggy trousers. A bus and a couple of cars had also stopped, their passengers squatting down to watch from the slope of the embankment.

Craig opened for England and soon knocked up quite a decent score. However, just as he was beginning to look irremovable, disaster struck. All the younger locals were playing barefooted, skipping about on the crazed, dried-up mud like lizards though their older teammates wore sandals. Craig, of course, had on trainers but his energetic toing and froing as he made his runs began to cut through the thin sun-dried crust, allowing a slippery ooze to flow onto the pitch. Poor Craig, one second the personification of commitment and acceleration; the next an unstable collection of flaying limbs at war with gravity. Twenty-six, run out. Alan next and he is short but sweet. Three mighty sixes and then he is caught in the outer field by a spectator who had ran onto the pitch. That, at any rate, was Alan's version. Umpire Roy, probably confused in his own mind as to who was a spectator and who a player, nonetheless gave Alan 'out', insisting that as the ball was returned to the bowler without it touching the ground, it was, technically, a catch! Dave Armstrong, wisely adapting to local conditions, took his stand barefoot and lasted long enough for the independent minded umpire to declare a draw on the grounds that both sides had enjoyed the same number of overs!

The final act was a shaking of hands all round and the presenting of the *'Jack Hatfield Signed Special'* and the unused pukka cricket ball to the village as mementoes of the match. Funnily enough, none of us thought to enquire what the village was called.

We found the offices of Katrak & Company buried among a tangle of warehouses and commercial properties just off Chundrigar Road, the heartland of Karachi's business area. For all Karachi's vast and chaotic sprawl, finding Chundrigar Road had occasioned no difficulty whatever and had simply been a matter of allowing ourselves to be swept along in an agitated current of gaudy buses and overloaded trucks that had gathered and begun to swell when we had first reached the city's outskirts. By the time we were running along Jinnah Road this current had become a tidal bore carrying all before it and we were lucky enough to be pitched involuntarily into a side stream to fetch up, breathless and bewildered but in one piece, in a safe haven. To our amazement a street sign attached to a nearby building read 'Chundrigar Road' – an astonishing navigational hole-in-one in a vast metropolis. Perhaps, indeed, a second miracle?

Katrak & Company occupied a great Mogul-gothic pile whose imposing entrance was handsomely adorned with white marble and well-polished brass – with a much-siring commissionaire thrown in for good measure. We were clearly expected and within seconds a decorous elderly clerk had ushered me into a noisy, iron-grilled lift which then baritone hummed its way floor past floor of busy clerks until it reached regions of panelled hardwood and thick carpets. There, with punctilious grace, I was introduced to Mr Katrak.

I saw at once as we shook hands that Jimmy Katrak was my mind's eye stereotypical company director: Stocky, balding, expensively grey-suited, neatly moustachedand fiftyish. He projected experience, ability and trust. I felt as might a storm-thrashed ship slipping at last past the breakwater and into a secure harbour.

"Nas Khan told my son all about your wonderful journey," he began, "and about your problems arising from the troubles in India. I was fascinated by your adventures and am eager to help. I am sure a solution viii be possible, but you must be a little patient. There are many things we must do but here in Karachi it is not quite like in London. Things take a little time."

"You must call me Jimmy," he continued, after he had taken a brief telephone call and waved me into a deep armchair. "All my friends do. I had this name at school. The minister you met, Nasir Khan; we were at school together."

"Well, I can hardly say how grateful we all are for this help. We are in quite a fix and I must say it is a relief to be able to explain our problems in English…"

"Of course, all business here is in English. Karachi is a very international city. All the children here want to learn English at school. My father sent me to school in Lahore. A British school. My children also. Now my sister's son, Ardevan, will start his A-levels next month in England. Anyway, you will meet all these people when we go to my house tomorrow."

We chatted over tea, covering many topics. Clearly Jimmy Katrak was urbane and well-read. And a bigshot too, for all the while secretaries and subordinates kept popping in for decisions or for papers to be signed. I snatched a brief glance at my watch, conscious of having left Roy and the boys suffocating in the parked bus for far too long.

"Don't worry, sir. Your boys are in our courtyard having some juice and I've got a fellow looking after your vehicle. I have, by the way, booked rooms for you at the Beach Luxury Hotel. It is not as central as some, but it is very comfortable and is convenient for this office. When you get there will you please take all your possessions into the hotel? About seven tomorrow morning I will send someone round to go with you to the port."

"I fear officials at the port," Jimmy Katrak went on, "will want you to sign all kinds of declarations. My man will help you but of course only you can sign. But you'll have no vorries. Everything the officials do is in English. I think this will all take a couple of hours. My man, of course, afterwards will take you back to the hotel. After that it will be possible for you to see something of Karachi. Oh and I nearly forgot. Once you have registered into the hotel you must let my man have all your passports because we need them to show to the people of the airline."

All these details whirled about me like torn-off branches in a hurricane. Each, separately, I could comprehend but where was the whole? What, in half a sentence, was the focus of it all? My busy host was now standing, his hand outstretched, poised for my courteous dismissal. A minion had already opened the door for me.

"I'm awfully sorry, Jimmy," I stammered. "I realise you are busy and I don't want to take any more of your time than I can help but I am totally in the dark over what is happening."

"I don't understand you. Surely the minister…did you not discuss everything with him?"

"No. We didn't really have time to discuss anything. He had a flight to Islamabad to catch and was very pushed for time. All he said was I should call on you when we got to Karachi as he thought you would be able to help us sort out the travel problem that the closed Indian frontier had caused."

"I see," he said slowly, shrugging expressively. "Well, the misunderstanding is of no importance. The minister, you see, has asked PNSC to find room on – PNSC is the Pakistan National Shipping Corporation – on the next sailing for your vehicle. There will be no charge for shipping your vehicle. My firm, you understand, are the agents for PNSC but the timetable of the ship is not suitable for you to travel…"

He hesitated, consulting a file and turning over some papers. "I'm afraid it does not sail until the end of next month. So, there is a difficulty we must look at. You and your boys will go separately by plane and Nasir Khan has already arranged this. My people are trying to make bookings as we speak but just now many people are wanting tickets with the road crossing being closed."

"I see. Well, things are certainly moving fast…" I stopped as a clammy wave of nausea and panic passed over me. God knows, I thought, what all this will cost despite the wonderful free shipping and flights. I was already borrowing from the boys' spending money simply to buy fuel for the bus. The school governors and the parents, I to Id myself, will go spare!

"I'm afraid that not being able to enter India by road at Amritsar means we have incurred costs we have not allowed for, Mr…er…Jimmy. I will have to contact the school and have funds sent out. How long will that take, do you think?"

"Oh, I wouldn't bother doing all that," Jimmy said, airily waving his hand. "My firm will settle the account at the hotel and whatever sums are needed for the stevedores, for wharfage and the port surveyors. We can also advance you money for your needs. We will then invoice you in England."

"Well, that's most kind and greatly appreciated. Would it be possible to telephone to England from this office? It is time I put the people at home in the picture. It is a long time since they have heard from us."

"Of course. But" he added, raising a cautionary finger in the air, "don't forget the time difference. It would be better to use the facilities at the hotel this evening. You will find them very efficient in such things."

The Beach Luxury Hotel certainly lived up to its title and must have been one of Karachi's very best hotels but the flip side, of course, lay in the scale of its charges. I could see that Jimmy Katrak's first thought would have been to see that we got decent accommodation and I didn't suppose for one moment that it would have occurred to him that our budget for sleeping, when it wasn't zero for some bare earth beneath the stars, would not normally have stretched beyond the meanest in town. However, I just didn't dare ask him to change us to somewhere much cheaper because, having already received so much generosity over the free flights to Bombay and the free shipping of the bus to the same destination, I was scared he would think I was fishing to have the accommodation paid as well.

In the end I decided to see if the manager of the hotel could come with any helpful ideas by letting him suppose that unless he gave us a special deal this one night was as long as we could afford to stay. Given the hotel's convenient location for Katrak & Co., I felt that they probably pushed quite a bit of business the hotel's way and that the hotel would be reluctant to see a friend of Jimmy depart for want of some modest amelioration of the tariff.

Jimmy Katrak had booked us six doubles. What if, I queried, this were cut back to three doubles and only charging according to the rooms occupied? This meant in effect the hotel turning a blind eye to how many boys we actually put in a room.

Initially the manager dismissed the idea out of hand, taking refuge in the fire regulations. In strict truth he may have had a point but when I upped my bid by suggesting he charged an extra ten percent on the room rate, the fire regulations lost their importance and a deal was struck. The boys, however, were apparently not best pleased by my necessary economy.

"I think, headmaster," began Roy rather diffidently a short while later, "you ought to be aware the boys are a bit upset by the room changes."

"Good heavens, why is that? They are still in the same hotel, with the same luxury rooms and showers and so on."

"Yes, but of course now they have only five beds so half of them will be on the floor."

"Poor little darlings! They've slept on the ground often enough, so where's the big deal? Anyway, the beds are huge for singles so if they don't like the floor they can share."

"Well, I just thought I would mention it."

"Well, I'm annoyed and you can tell them that. If there is one thing, I find pathetic it is great strapping lads fussing on about comfort. They can start worrying about cushions and their rheumatism when they're sixty."

I had to leave the boys in Roy's charge that evening and did not dine with them. Instead, I had my international phone calls to make. As the system then was, these had first to be pre-booked. After that you simply had to hang around until the exchange called you back and put you through, but this process was seldom quick and could easily involve a wait some hours. The first and most vital of my calls was to the school.

Naturally my good news concerning the wellbeing of the expedition and of its members was well received but the news given me in exchange was both shattering and yet curiously liberating. Its import centred on a telegram Lepra had recently sent to the school.

Around the time we had been making our way through the wilds of Baluchistan, a period of course where we had no means of communicating with the main cities of Pakistan, let alone with our folk back home in the United Kingdom, the school had received an urgent telegram from Lepra in India –

confirmed soon after by letter – announcing that the permission to import our minibus for donation to them had been revoked. The reason given by the Indian government was that surplus-to-requirements military vehicles were now being made available to appropriate charities by the Indian armed forces and therefore importation of donated vehicles was no longer considered to have any justification. Not knowing our exact whereabouts and so unable to contact us, the school's response had been to pass on the information to the British Consular offices in Amritsar, Karachi and Lahore in the expectation we would, at some stage, be almost certain to call in upon at least one of them. And so, we certainly would have had to do, had not Nasir Khan and Jimmy Katrak, by their fantastic kindness, made consular help unnecessary.

I saw at once that the Lepra telegram had altered the dynamics of the whole expedition. Sadly and very gallingly, our noble purpose in driving our old Transit all the way to India to help Lepra, albeit perhaps in a relatively minor way, perform their invaluable work had been rendered futile. In this regard I found it hard not to feel we had somehow failed in our basic endeavour. And yet, looking at the positive – which by nature I tend to do – I also saw that in every other respect we had achieved success. We had given the boys the once-in-a-lifetime adventure we had promised and, despite the odds stacked against us, we had indeed got our old bus as far as India. Additionally, in so doing we had very probably made a journey which in terms of adventure travel by a school group was up to that time unmatched.

Obviously, it was now quite pointless for Jimmy to continue to look for a way to ship our bus to Bombay. What I would now have to organise was for it and its trailer, to be shipped back to England to comply with the terms of its International *'Carnet de Passages en Douane'*. Pausing only long enough to telephone a couple of parents so that they could spread the word about our general well-being and imminent flight to Bombay, I hastened to find Roy and the boys so I could bring everyone up to speed regarding our changed circumstances. I located them, the lucky devils, cooling off in the hotel's rooftop pool.

"We ourselves still have to travel to India," I explained after they'd taken in the main facts "because our tickets to get back home, purchased long ago, are for from Delhi to Heathrow."

"They can't be changed?" asked Phil.

"Not at this late stage."

"Good," said Dave Armstrong. "I want to see some of India."

"How do we get to Delhi from Bombay, sir?" enquired James.

"By train. It may take two days. India is big and the trains are fairly slow."

And so, the questions kept coming but now that a definite programme was emerging and the feeling of being up a creek without a paddle was fading, my brave companions very quickly began to redisplay the buoyant spirit that had been so characteristic of our long journey.

Chapter 23

Next morning, I was up bright and early to be ready for the man that Jimmy Katrak had assigned to me to assist with the paperwork at the docks. However, now that England rather than Bombay was the required destination, my first priority had been to let Jimmy know about the change and hear what he had to say regarding the new situation. Apparently, he had not been planning to come into his office this particular morning and it took some time for his staff to track him down. We met just after 11 am.

To my surprise – and intense relief – Jimmy Katrak did not seem at all put out by my news that our minibus was not now be shipped to Bom bay. On the contrary, as he quickly made clear, PNSC had many more vessels engaged in trade with England and Europe than it did with Bombay and reminded me that the next PNSC sailing for Bombay could not have been until the end of September, a whole month away. But while sailings to England might be much more often, the sailing distance was vastly greater with, surely, proportionate differences in cost? Once again Jimmy astounded me with his optimism.

"Don't vorry yourself. I will talk about it to Nasir when we meet. Meanwhile, it is good that you go now to the docks with my man. The procedures are the same whatever the sailing destination."

But for the help of Jimmy Katrak's man I feel I might have still been at the docks a month later, so involved were the legal and maritime requirements and so labyrinthine were the procedures. Every stage involved batches of incomprehensible forms, all with an associated rash of carbon copies, fees, receipts, authorisations and approvals. Every stage, naturally, necessitated traipsing to a different off ice in a different part of the port, each with its own idiosyncratic opening hours. Even narcotics officials had to be talked to and driven down to vet the bus before customs would condescend to giving clearance for loading.

The tedium of all this bewildering bureaucracy, however, was small beer when set against the shear sweat and labour of physically preparing the bus for its voyage – work which I had not foreseen and for which I was unsuitably dressed and totally unprepared.

In his generous response to our inability to move forward into India at Amritsar in accordance with our planned itinerary, as already explained Mr Nasir Khan had arranged for our bus to be taken to Bombay by sea and for us, its passengers, to go by air to the same destination. Unhappily, he had either not noticed our trailer or had not remembered it, yet to fulfil the legal requirements the trailer also had to be exported from Pakistan. Mr Nasir Khan had ordered that we should be assigned a standard steel container in which to ship our vehicle, and this had been done, but as it occupied nine- tenths of the container, how on earth could we also accommodate the trailer?

Obvious solutions such as our paying for a second container were ruled out as quickly as I suggested them. The paperwork and customs had been done on the basis of one container and if two were involved all would have to be done again. Besides, Mr Khan's orders had been for one container and I soon sensed that no one was at all keen to meddle with instructions that had come from an important government minister.

Well then. I suggested, why not just sling the dratted trailer aboard and then lose it quietly in some remote corner of the ship? Sorry, the m.v. *Malran* was only able to accept containerised cargo.

An intriguing conundrum, if nothing else, I reflected bitterly. Perhaps just the thing for testing the wits of candidates at a Navy Selection Board but no joke for a forlorn and exhausted schoolteacher suffering the searing heat of Karachi. But, necessity, they say, is the mother of invention. Mulling over in my mind the troubles the trailer had caused us; I recalled the frustration of not being able to see it in the driving mirrors because of it being narrower than the bus. *Narrower than the bus!*

Eureka! If narrower than the bus, could it not be shipped *inside* it? Indeed, it could…just, but only, of course, if first all the seats were removed. And this 'but' was unfortunately a pretty grim one for it meant me scrabbling about underneath the vehicle in the dust and the dirt undoing the umpteen rusted-up bolts securing the seats to the floor.

Two hours and lots of bloodied knuckles later, despite victory over the seats, battle was still being done. This time it was with the luggage rack, its height infuriatingly making the bus too high by an inch to go into container. Flat tyres completed my victory.

That evening Mr and Mrs Katrak took us all to a superb open-air dinner at the Karachi Boat Club where we were introduced to some of the wider Katrak family and to some of Jimmy's business friends. The place had all the ambience and the no-expense spared amenities that a posh Home Counties golf club might offer. Jimmy also brought me the good news that Pakistan International Airlines had found seats for us on their Monday morning flight to Bombay.

"That gives you von more day in Karachi," he continued, "and I suggest you take your boys crab fishing in the harbour. The harbour of Karachi, you should know, is a true natural harbour and is very, very big. It is one of the biggest in Asia. The fishing harbour is part of it and there are mangrove swamps and many things to see. Crab fishing is good fun and your boys are sure to enjoy themselves."

"Well, that sounds a splendid idea. Is it easy for you to arrange though?"

"Very easy. Leave it to me. I will send cars round to your hotel to pick you up."

"Ten thirty? That will not be too early?"

"Gosh no. But are you sure? You have already done so much for us that…"

Our host silenced me with a peremptory wave of his hand. "Now you must come," he said, throwing an arm round me, "and tell my sister Vera and her husband all about English sixth-forms and which school might be best for Ardevan to attend when he goes to England."

The occasion of the Boat Club dinner was also a night to remember for a reason unconnected with Jimmy Katrak's generosity and lavish hospitality. Up to this moment in all our long and challenging travels no one had been troubled by anything beyond the mildest of stomach disorders. This was an amazing record given the rough and ready arrangements we lived by and owed much, in my view, to the rugged fitness of boys obliged by school policy to participate in a good deal of sport and physical activity. For their part the boys affected to believe, especially if they thought I might be listening, that their gastric hardiness arose from constant exposure to school food! The Karachi Boat Club's upmarket cuisine bore little resemblance to either school lunches or the renderings of our camp cooking but some element within its overall excellence may have been flawed. Or, perhaps, something as simple as the water of the hotel's swimming pool may have been to blame. At all events, for whatever reason, several boys were disturbingly ill during that night and no one escaped altogether unaffected. However, youthful constitutions and quick recovery usually go hand-in-hand and by breakfast time, despite a welter of bleary eyes from lost sleep, everyone pronounced himself ready for the great crab-fishing adventure.

Karachi crab-fishing boats, save for a cramped accommodation cabin towards the stern, are open decked, crudely planked affairs. Shaped in plan like a domestic clothes iron, these simple craft are of low freeboard for their entire length of twenty or so feet. An ancient engine, clanking noisily away amidships, is responsible for whatever laboured progress around the murky brown harbour waters the boat manages to achieve. Our vessel's crew of three, also murky brown and ragged to a degree that was virtually indecent, comprised a toothless ancient at the helm, a scraggy bloke with horrid boils all down his bare arms, who hung around the bow area and a boy who, at the moment of our arrival on board, was busily cleaning out the spaces between his toes. We later discovered that this lad's principal role was to make tea and generally see to the food. Once underway, the fellow with the boils called us over to explain the technicalities of the fishing gear. He had no English, but the simplicity of the arrangements enabled us to get the hang of things readily enough. The first essential was to fix a scrap of putrid meat to a weighted length of string and the second, which completed the preparations, was to lower the resulting apparatus into the water.

Sooner or later and in the main it was surprisingly soon, the fisher would feel a gentle tug on his line. Now came the critical bit: A few inches at a time the line had to be hauled back until, if you had been gentle enough, you would find a large leggy crustacean thrashing about on the end of your string.

It was at this point the ship's boy came into his own. Yelling in enthusiastic glee, he would rush over and heroically ignoring the fearsome-looking claws and pincers, seize the beady-eyed creature in his hands. Then, to the hideous sound of tearing and crunching, the writhing, living object would be wrenched apart, limb by limb, before its dismembered body and larger limbs were tossed into a bucket of boiling water. It was certainly no sight for the squeamish and I caught a couple of boys screwing up their faces and averting their gazes from the horror of it all.

"Sir, where is the toilet?"

"Toilet? Toilet," I repeated vacuously as I strove to tear my mind away from the continuous butchery of the caught crabs. "I'm sorry laddie but I doubt there's any such thing on a boat like this. If you are desperate, you'll have to go discreetly over the side."

"That's no good, sir. It's urgent. I *need* somewhere where I can *sit.*"

Obviously upset and close to tears with embarrassment, the youngster's distress must have been noticed by the helmsman for he abruptly called out and held an enamel bucket up in the air. As I took it and passed it over, the poor lad gave the filthy befouled object one glance and all but passed out.

"Hold on laddie," I said gently, abandoning the bucket and steering him towards the back of the boat where a simple bench lined the stern rail. "Hang on tight and don't overbalance, but just sit on the rail and stick your bottom overboard and you'll be OK."

"But the crew and everyone, sir. They'll —"

"Never mind them. Tomorrow you'll be in India and they'll be here."

At one stage a little later there were three white bottoms hanging in a row over the stern of the 'Lotus', which would have presented a highly unusual sight had another vessel been closely following. At the same time sundry other unhappy-looking youngsters were leaning over the side amidships in more conventional postures of maritime distress and one, naked from the waist down, was busy laundering his shorts.

It was at this point the crew called us over to enjoy our self-harvested meal of crab and salad.

Chapter 24

It is a frightening thing to look on while youngsters for whom you are *'in loco parentis'* fall ill in circumstances you can do little to remedy, especially when feeling pretty ropey yourself. And to be honest, I certainly do wonder if my own head masterly dignity would have survived intact had a personal performance over the stern rail been required! Of course, if I had been a dutiful and politically correct health and safety fellow, then I would not have dreamt in the first place of taking pupils aboard a ship or boat of any description without being armed with a prescribed medical kit and a file of counselling leaflets. But then, if I had been a politically correct health and safety freak would I have exposed pupils to the perils of anything resembling adventure?

"Everything OK this morning?" I asked a smiling youngster as I shuffled up the airliner steps behind him.

"Oh yes, sir. I think everyone is fine now thanks to that Lomotil stuff Danny and Mr Woodforde dished out last night and again this morning."

"Which is just as well isn't it?" Chipped in the lad behind me before a fit of uncontrolled smirky laughter took possession of him.

"Let us all share the joke," I said turning. There was a sea of expectant eyes looking on, but no one seemed anxious to explain. "Well?" I prompted.

It was Slackie who at length obliged. "Well, sir, the method you told us to use on the boat wouldn't work with an airliner. That's…" he shrugged before finishing. "Well, we all thought the idea of doing it from a plane, well, funny. That's all."

My pitying smile and raised eyebrows seemed to close the subject.

"Well Roy," I remarked as I eased myself into the seat next to his. "They're all back in top form and fine spirits if their inane conversations are anything to go by. I wonder how things will go in India."

"Badly if there's any justice."

"Eh? Good Lord, what makes you say that?"

"Well, in one way and another we've had so many scrapes and disasters that have turned out fine in the end that it would not be fair on the rest of mankind if such luck were to last for ever."

I mulled over Roy's remark for quite a time and in a sulky spirit too for a while. Was he getting at me? I let the various incidents in our journey flash through my mind like a flipped through picture book.

"You may have a point, Roy," I conceded. "Whatever else you need for a crazy scheme to succeed, you certainly need luck."

We were standing in the exit area of Bombay Airport, each of us lumbered with a heavy rucksack, feeling bemused and doubtless looking it when a sharp-eyed tout summed up our situation and swung into action. I had been warned by Jimmy Katrak to steer clear of such folk by relying on the airline help desk but having no idea of where we might stay or how we might get to the city centre I though the opportunistic tout was worth a hearing.

It was a lucky move. The man, dressed in typical Bombay 'whites', spoke fair English and explained he was working for an Indian ex-servicemen's charity, raising funds and helping with their employment by running taxis and hire buses. He looked and sounded genuine and on a spur of the moment decision! Hired for the day the little bus he had parked just outside the airport exit. I first asked him to take us to a suitable hotel and then afterwards to give us a tour of the city. Hassan, the jovial and chatty driver he assigned to us, was a mine of information and, speaking excellent English, knew just where to go to give us the best possible coverage of the great city in the very limited time available to us.

However, I must say he made very heavy weather over his first task, namely, to find us an economical hotel. As a first shot he drove up to the 'Taj Mahal Intercontinental' and was, I think, genuinely surprised when we told him it was not the sort of place we had in mind, being way above our budget.

"You must not vorry," he said. "I go in and get for you, two respected English gentlemen, a very good price. They know me here. Many times, I get special price for my people."

It proved amazingly difficult to get into Hassan's head that though we trusted we made the grade as 'English gentlemen' nonetheless we really were looking for somewhere cheap and cheerful and when we settled on the Hotel Kamal, a dilapidated hostelry in an area where most of the buildings were bandaged by lines of drying washing, it took the poor fellow at least five minutes to stop shaking his head in disbelief. We were able to hire two four-bedded rooms and one two-bedded, leaving it to an unlucky pair to choose between sharing or taking to the floor and risking the wildlife.

"Hurry up chaps," I called, ignoring a lively argument raging between Tom, James, Danny and Squeak as to which choice should prevail.

"Take what you'll need for a day in the city. We'll leave everything else here. Don't forget to take your passports as Mr Woodforde will need them when we go to the station to book the train."

"But sir, will it be safe to leave our stuff here?" Demanded Adrian.

"Well, it may not be Fort Knox, but it will be a darned sight safer than traipsing round the city with a thumping great rucksack."

"But the bedroom doors don't have locks, sir."

"Gosh, you're right. I hadn't noticed."

However, the problem was soon overcome by the obliging hotel owner promising to fit hasps and padlocks while we were out.

Bombay (or *Mumbai* in more recent years), with a population of at least 15 million, is India's largest city and in commercial terms its most important. Before the era of air travel, people journeying to India from Europe of course did so by sea and the Gateway of India, a huge yellow basalt archway dominating the dock area of Bombay, gave them their first sight of India. It seemed a good point to commence our own tour.

The nearby Sassoon Dock is the home of Bombay's coastal fishing fleet and watching the morning unloading of the previous night's catch gave us a show which for colour and raucous human activity would have bested anything that the imagination of the most gifted impresario could have dreamt up. Whilst in the same *Colaba Causeway* area we were overwhelmed by the amazing wealth of street-based restaurants and food stalls; surely one of the most exotic, extensive and diverse epicurean centres on earth. The striking Victorian church of St. John, built in 1847 was also briefly toured before we took a hasty lunch in the open along Marine Drive, a great curving promenade looking out onto the Arabian Sea.

Next in our impossibly hectic see-Bombay-in-a-day itinerary was a tour of the *Maidan,* making a special point of looking at the buildings of Bombay University and of the High Court, both typical of the many imposing buildings erected during the city's period of great growth under the British Raj. The favoured style is Gothic and the Rajabai Clock Tower, 250 feet tall, dominates the area much as Big Ben does Westminster. The city's two main railway stations, Bombay Victoria and Bombay Central, are both serious rivals to London's St Pancras in Gothic splendour. As we had to visit Central anyway to book our tickets for next day's journey to Agra, we made a virtue of necessity and included these gorgeous examples of Victorian railways in our sightseeing.

Next it was back to Marine Drive and then up to Malabar Hill where there is a Jain temple of quite extraordinary gaudiness. Malabar Hill also affords excellent views of Bombay. One part of the city I did not have on my itinerary was a trip down Falkland Street to *The Cages,* but our driver had us there before I had cottoned on to what the place was. This is the city's posher Red-Light district. The boys seemed most chuffed over being taken to see such a 'grown up' sight and according to Roy, as a result my stock had risen in their eyes!

The final item on our frenetic round of sightseeing was a visit to the city laundry – a bizarre choice on the face of things but in fact a most fascinating experience. Bombay's *dhobi ghat* enables over five thousand *dhobi wallahs* to wash and beat thousands of articles of clothing in a vast township of concrete troughs and tanks.

Brought each morning from all over the city, the tons of clothing involved are separated and then washed according to their colour and fabric. The washing comprises two principal processes: First a soaking in soapy water for two or three hours; and then, the beating out of the dirt. You may believe it, or you may not, but the plain fact is that no wonder washing machine incorporating the latest technology as sold by the likes of Currys or Argos to Persil-besotted British housewives comes halfway towards achieving so good a job. Close by the *dhobi ghat* are the drying fields where miles and miles of line are used to subject the newly washed clothes to the fierce rays of the Indian sun. Then it is onto the ironing sheds where hundreds of toiling women, employing the most primitive of irons, press the clothes as you've never seen clothes pressed before. Even socks are given razor-edged creases fore and aft like mini trouser legs.

The whole show provides the best industrial visit you are ever likely to make, far surpassing such soulless experiences as seeing round an automated no-people-anywhere-at all car factories. You see, the *dhobi ghat* achieves a daily human miracle the like of which, even today, no sinister Orwellian identity checking computer could manage. How so? Well, bearing in mind all those thousands of garments and items of household linen are washed according to colour and fabric and are *NOT* kept together by ownership, nevertheless at the end of it all each customer receives back *exactly* what was sent!

Oh and just to say in case you think you have solved the riddle of the Bombay washing miracle, no; you do not need to have your laundry name-tabbed, marked, or numbered.

By and large Indian trains are not fast, their journeyings having more in common with the solid reliability of the camel that the skittish dashing's of a greyhound.

Established travel writers like to talk of discovering 'the *soul* of a country' and, if I have correctly understood the full nuances of their meaning, then I would say you certainly get India for real when you travel by rail. The image most people harbour when thinking of India's railways is of carriages packed to bursting, invariably with still more folk hanging on the outside around the doors and steps and with bunches of intrepid youths madly travelling on the carriage roofs. And yes, there are trains which match this picture, but these are the commuter trains serving cities such as Calcutta or Bombay.

Such an image is perhaps unfair to what is typical of India's forty-thousand-mile network. Very much reflecting its labyrinthine social system, the travel classes and levels of comfort on Indian railways are a complex matter to say the least of it. First, there are classes of *train* to think about. A *passenger* train is to be avoided at all costs. It will stop at every station and be subject to interminable delays. What you want is either a *mail* train or an *express;* the latter label, however, covering status and having little to do with speed. There are at least half a dozen gradings of comfort though few trains will offer the full range. More or less at the top is 'Reserved 1st class air-conditioned sleeper'; a good deal cheaper is a 1st class sleeper without air-conditioning (and without bedding). In this class the beds are two-tier, there being four berths to each compartment, the two top berths folding away in daytime to create a spacious four-place day saloon. Second-class sleepers are three-tier and are arranged in doorless sections of six berths. There are also chair-only carriages on some trains with air-conditioned first, first and second classes, all these being fitted out with airline-style seating. Such trains are invariably overcrowded and noisy. Third class, which is something else, is also available on some trains.

Despite the chaotic bustle at departure, everything worked out fine and we quickly settled down into our three compartments. Indian carriages are hugely commodious in comparison with those that serve the British Isles and after the cramped seating of the minibus the train felt distinctly luxurious. Air-conditioned First Class is obviously a nice little indulgence, but it would have been significantly more expensive than the ordinary First we had gone for and truly beyond our means. Besides, all those weeks spent in the minibus had hardened us to the heat and we were more than happy to sit by the open window drinking in the scenery. Our fresh air habit, however, worried the conductor, who saw it as a security risk and to keep him happy we travelled at night with the louvered shutters lowered.

Mealtimes were interesting to say the least. Rather like the practice in many British hospitals, a steward would come round many hours ahead of the meal to make up his order. The first decision required of you was to decide whether you were to be *vegetarian* or *non-vegetarian* as the menu cards handed out reflected this basic divide. The menu cards had plainly been typed several at a time by means of inter-leafed carbon paper and were terribly difficult to decipher for all that they were bilingual with English as the dominant print. However, as the wording in English and that in the local Indian language had had to be done on a different typewriter, misalignments as scripts were transferred from machine to machine meant many menu items were unreadable due to unintended superimposition of one language on top of the other!

The boys made much of the luxury of menu choice and spent a good deal of time studying and deciphering the menu and consulting one another over their choices. The steward, a man with the patience of Job, did not appear to be at all put out by this youthful procrastination, solemnly noting down each long-debated choice and calmly coping with never-ending amendments. When lunch duly arrived at about two-thirty, each diner received a large stainless-steel tray, called a *dabba,* which had dents or depressions pressed into it to provide separate places for each chosen item. The idea was to balance the tray on your knee and tuck in, the only snag being that the tray was far too hot to hold in comfort, so rucksacks had to be hastily raided for towels or other means of thermal insulation. This slight delay gave each fellow a chance to study what his neighbours had selected and perhaps reflect the wisdom of his own choices. But here was a fine to do for all the *dabbas* were identical and thus all the agonised effort put into the selection process had been so much wasted effort. In due course the used *dabbas* were collected and stacked up in the exit vestibule of the carriage and I began to see how the system worked.

Once the menu choices had been made, the steward must have left the details at the first station stop so that they could be telephoned down the line ahead of the train. On arrival at a subsequent station, the meals, already 'trayed-up' and individually identified, would have then been put on the train. Clearly the final stage was going to be the off-loading of the used trays for washing and return to the system when the train next stopped. Mildly interested in seeing if my conjecture was correct, I made a point of being by the door when the next station was reached. Sure enough, the steward gathered up the yard-high pile of *dabbas* and noisily rattled and clanged his way across the platform before setting down his load. Wiping his hands on some tissues salvaged from his trays, he then turned round to make his way back towards the train. As he did so a great pack of dogs came racing into view and in the blink of an eye, they had descended upon the stack of discarded *dabbas,* scattering them like a fan of cards before launching themselves into an ecstasy of tray licking interspersed with brief interludes of snarling and quarrelling. Did the K-9 process just witnessed, I could not help wondering, constitute the whole cycle of washing prior to the *dabbas* being gathered together for reuse?

As we emerged ruck-sack laden from the gloomy portals of Agra Cantonment station into the dazzling afternoon sunlight we were instantly ambushed by swarms of touts. each fanatically determined to snatch us away to the hotel that commissioned his hunting. Applying good Darwinian principles, I selected the noisiest and most aggressive to handle our business and was pleased to learn that our man represented an affordable hotel within walking distance, but it was his offer personally to carry my rucksack for me that actually clinched the deal. The Grand Hotel, although undoubtedly in a superior league to our abode in Bombay, fell somewhat short of its self-chosen title but was nonetheless adequate and had the bonus of a pleasant garden.

One of the peripheral benefits of travelling with schoolboys in Arab countries and though much of the Orient is that within the indigenous cultures and traditions, sons – and by extension boys in general – are held in especial regard. The arrival of a party of foreign boys is therefore seen as good news as far as the locals are concerned, people often falling over themselves in their eagerness to be friendly and helpful. At all events the manager of the Grand Hotel Agra, a small bald fellow with enormous thick-framed spectacles, could not hide his delight that we had singled out his establishment and at once abandoned his mundane duties to attend in person to the needs of his English princelings. Hands were peremptorily clapped in oriental style and instantly there were servants scurrying about seeing to our luggage whilst others served us with tiny sugar-frosted glasses of ice-cold fruit juice. Far from being dismayed, as might well an

English hotel manager, that a bunch of dishevelled travel- stained youths, rivalling a darts team in the paucity of their social graces, were knocking back his cordials two glasses at a time, our host stirred himself into a flurry of further hand clapping and servant summoning. Even the calamity of an inverted tray and smashed glasses, provoked by greedy snatching, did nothing to stem his extravagant bonhomie.

The plumbing upstairs was no match for the effusiveness below. The uncompromising two-way choice in my shower between a scalding trickle of clear water and a modest flow of lukewarm brown seemed reasonable enough given the hotel's tariff but what was harder to accept was the acute tingling experienced in reaching up to re-angle the rose of the electric shower head. Fearing the hotel might harbour showers with still more dramatic side-effects, I shouted to Roy and asked him to race round and stop the boys showering until we had made some safety checks. Bare supply cables vulnerable to spray and splashes proved to be a feature of every installation and a shower regime restricted to cold water usage was duly decreed. Three boys, who had finished showering before the ban claimed they had enjoyed really hot water with the added novelty of miniature lightning flashes in the steamy clouds above their heads. Accompanying thunder was not mentioned.

On learning that our proposed itinerary would not stretch beyond two nights in Agra, Ronnie Corbett (as the hotel maitre, Mr Prasad, had been instantly christened) was quick to voice his disappointment.

"You come to see the most beautiful building in the world," he grumbled, "and you say you will give it only a few hours. What kind of experience for these young men is that? The Taj is a temple to love. Love is not for just the daytime. You must also see the Taj at night when there is moon and also in the early morning when there is the special light of the new day. These are the times when love is most strong. Do you not understand?"

He was berating me in the foyer where I had told the boys to assemble prior to our setting out to visit the bazaars and to get ourselves a meal. Naturally they were all ears and loving every moment of my discomfiture.

"How can we go at night?" I retorted. "The guidebook says it closes at sunset."

"Aa...ah!" Our hotelier cried, wagging a finger at me in belligerent contradiction.

"Is it now? Let me ask you, sir, do you and your young friends want to see the Taj when it is full and crowded like a bazaar? Or do you want to see it when it is quiet and it is a place of dreams?"

It turned out that his brother-in-law happened to work as a guide at the Taj and for a small supplement added to the normal entrance charge it appeared that we could be smuggled inside in the small hours and have the privilege of experiencing the Taj sunrise all to ourselves long before the public got there.

"What happens if we are caught getting in?" asked the ever-practical James.

The gravity of the question seemed to delight the little man with the big glasses and once his extravagant chuckles had subsided, he suddenly threw an arm round James.

"My friend, you ask a very good question," he purred in a mock-serious tone. "Did you know that the favourite punishment of the great Moghul emperors, like the one who built the Taj, was to have those who trespassed in their harems trampled to death by trained elephants? What do you think of that?"

James, already lobster-red at being singled out for the hotelier's embrace, clearly thought little and was saying less.

"Today, that way would be thought too messy, I think," our host continued. "Perhaps today," he added, throwing his hands together and miming an executioner's stroke, "the guards just cut off your head with their swords."

James seized the moment of the mime to make his escape, doing so with such expressive alacrity that we all roared with laughter while Mr Prasad, believing his remarks to be the source of our humour, bounded about in a transport of delight, hugging anyone he could corner. It seemed to me a good moment to fix a deal.

"Right chaps. What do you say to risking the elephant death and going in for this pre-dawn admission that Mr Prasad has offered?"

The suggestion was hailed with enthusiasm.

The sky was hazy and grey as we made our way through silent streets towards the Taj at just before five. As instructed, I knocked at a small door to the right of the Taj Mahal's western entrance and, after a short delay, it was opened to the tune of drawn bolts and rattled chains. A soldier with a grim face loomed out of the shadows and for one scary moment I thought the arrangements had miscarried.

"The school from England, yes?" asked a thin, turbaned man in a crumpled white suit who had abruptly sidled into view.

To our surprise, instead of beckoning us to enter, our guide led us down a lane running outside the wall of the Taj towards the river – the river Yamuna. Two boats, each in the charge of a young boy, were waiting and minutes later we were gliding across at an angle towards the far bank. The river was smooth and black with no discernible current and inches above it a veil of mist hovered, making the boats appear wraith-like as if skating on the water rather than floating in it. We fetched up on the far bank with the gentlest of nudges, finding ourselves in a field opposite the Taj.

Almost at the same moment the orange orb of the sun began to show, seeming to rise out of the river, its golden fingers caressing the Taj until the building appeared to be magically floating on a cloud of white vapour. It was nearly six before we got back to the small door by the main entrance and already a short queue of people waiting to go in had formed.

The dawn view of the Taj from its imposing gateway is truly stunning and is withheld until the very last step is taken, thus doubling the impact. Then, suddenly before you at the end of a long, avenue-like pool of clear water in which the Taj is beautifully reflected, lies Shah Johan's glorious pearly-white Temple to Love. The Taj Mahal's throat-lumping ethereal beauty as a distinct whole building masterpiece is matched by the exquisite execution of *its* details. For a start, the basic material of the mausoleum itself is dazzling white Makrana marble, with yellow or black marble being added where geometric patterns call for contrast. Then, all this sumptuous material is further enhanced by the lavish application of fine inlay, whereby turquoise from Tibet, agate from the Yemen, amethyst from Persia, sapphire from Ceylon, malachite from Russia, Chinese jade and Arabian coral are decoratively embedded in flowing patterns of breathtaking precision. The totality not only inspires awe and amazement: It leaves one wondering whether one is looking at architecture or at jewellery on a prodigious scale.

As one might well guess, the glittering glories of the Taj Mahal have balancing shadows and sadness's. The Moghul emperor Shah Jahan commenced building the Taj in 1631 in memory of his cherished wife and inseparable companion Mumtaz Mahal 'the Chosen One', who had died during the birth of her fourteenth child. It is said that as she lay dying, she asked the emperor to build something which would show the world how great was their love for one another. The task occupied twenty thousand workmen twenty-two years, specialist craftsmen being drawn from all over Asia and even from France and Italy. The main architect was Persian.

The expense of it all, the inconsolable ruler's neglect of his empire and total preoccupation with his building projects led to a palace coup in which he was overthrown. Imprisoned in Agra fort, the grief-stricken fallen emperor spent the last eight years of his life looking through a little prison window which gave him a restricted and distant view of his wife's resting place.

The boys' reaction to the splendours of the Taj and to the love story underpinning it varied enormously and they argued fiercely about it. I found it interesting that those specialising in arts subjects, or planning to when older, related particularly well to the sorrowfulness of the heartbroken Shah Jahan whereas the science types tended to be moved by the building itself and the scale of the works required to construct it. Adrian, for example, who had Design Technology as one of his A-levels, had been bowled over by the flawless precision of the inlay work but thought Johan's abandonment of his duties as a ruler 'most odd' and his behaviour 'soppy'!

Whatever their individual take on the Taj at dawn, all had enjoyed it enough to want me to ask our hotelier to make a similar arrangement so we could experience the Taj by moonlight. We spent most of the rest of the day touring the Red Fort, second only to the Taj in Agra's hierarchy of impressive historical sights. A strong demand from the troops for the bazaar to be briefly visited left us with only half an hour to snatch a meal before making our way back to the Taj. Our clandestine adventure in the moonlit night soon had us keyed up and jumpy and it seemed to me our guide was himself on edge and uncertain, as if he wasn't fully sure that he was going to get away with his little scheme a second time. He certainly rushed us round at breakneck speed as if he couldn't get rid of us fast enough and became distinctly agitated whenever anyone chanced to make an unnecessary noise. At the end he quibbled about the agreed baksheesh, saying that at night there were more guards and therefore more people for him to pay.

Nonetheless we did get away with it and did enjoy the rare privilege of seeing the Taj by moon light.

It had certainly been a very long day and by the time everyone was settled and I could collapse into bed it was virtually two in the morning. Roy and I had therefore been escorting, accompanying, supervising – call it what you will – for almost twenty-one hours on the trot. Not bad for two schoolmasters supposedly 'on holiday'.

Chapter 25

It was three-tier bunks and all the other privations of Indian Second-Class travel for our journey from Agra to Delhi. The Expedition funds were now in deficit and to keep us going I was borrowing pocket money from the few boys who still had any, so every penny counted. The train was jampacked, noisy and bordering on the riotous but we loved it for giving us such intimate glimpses into Indian life. I always feel that railways, especially when cutting through cities and urban sprawl, offer cheeky and privileged backyard views: Almost as if the tops of the houses have been lifted off to see what goes on inside. Roads, by contrast, run alongside front doors and the elevations designed to impress or deceive.

The train took about five hours to reach Delhi and when its tracks weren't running through an endless succession of rice fields on a flat and featureless landscape, they were picking their way through what must be some of the vilest slums on the face of the earth. The giant thermometer outside New Delhi railway station proclaimed our arrival temperature as 46°C, which we could well believe but as the adjacent clock had clearly stopped, we had to accept the evidence of our watches that we had reached the capital of the world's most populous democracy at precisely 2pm on Saturday 1st September 1984.

The day happened to be my birthday but headmasters, if they are wise, do not make known such information to their pupils. A headmaster friend of mine, unwise in this particular regard, was in consequence saddled with the arrival of a Birthday Kissogram delivered in person by a scantily clad young hussy in the middle of his morning assembly! But, back to Delhi...

We had arrived, it seemed to me, with the mindset of a bunch of wandering migrants. All our possessions were on our backs and in thirteen hours' time our flight back to England would be taking off from Delhi International, an airport infamous for the criminal inconvenience of its departure times. And was there tworse than three o'clock in the morning? Allowing a tight three hours to get from New Delhi to the airport and through all the passport hoo-ha, we had precisely ten hours to kill and a negative amount of money with which to do it.

Determined not to spend it in the environs of New Delhi station, we brushed aside the heart-rending entreaties of hotel touts, shoeshine boys, taxi drivers and various novel categories of 'me-fix-you-mister' and struck a bargain with four auto- rickshaws.

"Which hotel. Sahib?"

"No hotel. Just take us to the exact centre of the city if you please."

"That will be Connaught Place, sahib. You want to go there?"

"If you say so."

Short of tackling the Monaco Grand Prix Formula One car racecourse in the opposite direction to the rest of the cars, it is hard to imagine an urban motor adventure with more heart-stopping scares than a ride in one of Delhi's auto-rickshaws through the thick of the city's dense tangle of traffic. Of course, most major cities offer their own characteristic and specific traffic challenges. In Amsterdam it will be the excess of bold cyclists, in Athens the smoky buses, in Naples Lambretta-riding prostitutes and so on. Delhi's speciality is an omnipresence of all known species of road user in a perpetual kaleidoscope of instantly changing caprices. Locally cloned flag- displaying Morris Oxfords, assigned to political and ministerial grandees, slice their way through the traffic with speed and arrogance of attitude appropriate to couriers of the Genghis Khan. Delhi's buses are likely to stop without warning in whatever traffic lane to disgorge passengers through both left and right-sided exits. Clusters of cyclists, presumably believing there is safety in numbers, as often as not proceed in the opposite sense to the motorised traffic. Handcarts, pushed along by the Herculean efforts of skinny peasants, unable to see beyond their immensely bulky loads, cut at right angles across one lane after another. The many animals and horse-drawn vehicles, of course, have their very own enigmatic agendas, these generally becoming apparent a split second ahead of an irretrievable emergency. Unflinching pedestrians, mingling serenely among the fastest traffic is another of Delhi's specialities, as are bunches of street children rubbing shoulders with the hub caps of giant lorries.

The notable characteristic of the auto-rickshaw in the maelstrom of wandering missiles that is Delhi's traffic, is its amazing manoeuvrability and seeming knack of side-stepping out of trouble like a good wing three-quarter. Having four auto rickshaws at their service and psychologically responding, dare I say to the idiosyncratic individualism inherent in Delhi's traffic, the boys were quick to see a rickshaw race as an interesting possibility. Given the usual schoolboy panache for conjuring mischief and the competitive freebooting spirit of the young rickshaw drivers, perhaps I should not have been surprised. Initially I put down the increase in speed and the wilder, more reckless overtaking to the fact that we had reached an area of broader, more open streets but my eyes were opened to the true situation when we began to travel four abreast with the boys half-standing up whilst holding on for dear life and cheering like mad. It was impossible to make my voice heard to do anything about it and when I tapped my driver on his shoulder with a view at least to the withdrawal of my rickshaw from the madness, he mistook my purpose and redoubled his efforts to get ahead. Our sweeping turn from the road through the park into the first of the concentric circular avenues' characteristic of the Connaught Place area would have done credit to Ben-Hur, yet the pace hotted up still more as we screamed round the tight radius of the traffic circus marking the centre of Connaught Place itself. A flurry of generous tipping, warm handshakes, patted backs and laughter-split faces seemed proof enough that all conspirators, brown and white, had enjoyed their devilment.

We had stepped out of our chariots close to the Hotel Metro in Janpath Street and to any third-party observer must have seemed a pretty unprepossessing bunch of noisy scruffs standing by a heap of untidy luggage. However, to the hotel's go-getting manager, Mr Mehra, we clearly represented a business opportunity not to be missed.

"Were we", he eagerly enquired, dashing down the steps of the hotel's entrance as fast as his short baggy-trousered legs would allow, "looking for a hotel?"

"Not really," I replied in deliberately disinterested tones. "We will be heading to the airport in a few hours."

"So?" he queried, conjuring an expression of utter incredulity. "So, until then you walk the hot streets with all…with all this?" He finished with a sweeping wave embracing the boys and the luggage as if all were part of the same problem. Which, of course, were I to admit it, in a way they were!

"Sir, leave Delhi with happy memories. My hotel is at your service."

I settled on hiring two rooms, giving ourselves a place for our possessions, showers and four beds to rest upon. Even better, the excellent Mr Mehra told me that he would be very happy to cash a cheque for me – not only to settle the bill but also with enough to spare to allow us a taxi or two to give ourselves a chance of seeing something of Delhi. A late meal at around ten o'clock? Delighted to oblige! And to book a minibus to take us to the airport at one o'clock in the morning? But of course. No trouble at all!

Old Delhi, about three miles from Connaught Place, is the 17th century walled city that Shah Johan, our old friend from the Taj Mahal, created when he set out to move the capital of Mughal India from Agra to Delhi. It seemed to me that to go there and briefly look round the Red Fort, Old Delhi's most notable sight, would be a worthwhile way of spending the early part of the afternoon. Within the fort are several marble palaces and just to the north of it is the Kashmir Gate, famous in the Mutiny for the desperate fighting around it and for the heroism and sacrifice displayed there by both sides. To my surprise, this talk of visiting the Red Fort sparked off the beginnings of a second Indian mutiny.

"Oh sir, do we *have* to go?" Wailed Slackie when I outlined the plan. "I didn't sleep a wink last night and I'd just like to stay here and take it easy in the hotel."

"You seemed fresh enough on the train this morning," I observed tartly. David didn't reply but looked sulky.

"I agree with Slackie, sir," said Alan. "I think we're all pretty wacked out."

"Pretty pathetic, don't you think, Mr Woodforde?" Roy wisely maintained a studied and silent neutrality.

"I feel OK," said Adrian, "but I don't want to go touring around. It looks quite interesting around here. Is there a chance of a bit of free time instead, sir?"

"Hear, hear!" exclaimed Craig, his voice sounding clear above a general hubbub of support.

The trouble was I had painted myself into a corner and I felt guilty that I hadn't even consulted Roy, let alone any of the boys, before announcing my plans. On the other hand, I was annoyed that the boys were being awkward and I couldn't bring myself to be gracious.

"What have you to say about these poor *tired* children, Mr Woodforde?"

"I don't mind staying around in the hotel if that helps."

I didn't deserve such a prompt rescue, but I seized it with both hands. "Excellent, Mr Woodforde. We will divide. Those who want to see the glories of Old Delhi can come with me and the rest can remain here."

"But what about those of us who want to just look around the shops and stuff near here?" persisted Adrian.

"If you mean within a few hundred yards of the hotel, I imagine Mr Woodforde will OK it. But it's up to him."

Only Tom, James and Jason were loyal to my plan and came with me to Old Delhi.

All the rest had joined the mutiny!

I had also arranged for us all to go to take a look at Imperial Delhi, timing the occasion close to sunset when the great buildings of state are often dramatically silhouetted against a red-gold sky. Again, via the excellent Mr Mehra, I had pre- ordered transport, once again reserving four auto rickshaws, but this time, spoil sport that I am, getting him to make clear to the drivers that sedate and safe locomotion was desired. I had felt it important educationally for my young charges to witness at first hand the British role in India's development as a nation and, not being one who believes dogs should decide which vet to go to, I was prepared to be firm about our going as a complete group. However, in the extraordinary way that schoolboys have of coming up with the unexpected, they fell in with the idea as cheerfully as they would a cancelled detention!

It was in 1911 at the Delhi Durbar that the King – Emperor George V announced that the capital of India was to move from Calcutta to Delhi. A new city, initially covering thirty square miles, but having boundless possibilities for future expansion, would be created to the south of what henceforth would be known as 'Old Delhi'. Old Delhi itself, of course, was an amalgam of a series of cities established over the centuries by successive conquering powers. The First World War delayed things somewhat and it was not until 1931 that the new city was inaugurated. George V had wanted an architectural style similar in form and flavour to the Mughal masterpieces of Old Delhi and Agra but in the end, it was a suggestion of Lord Hardinge, the Viceroy, to have a style which married 'Western architecture to Oriental motifs' that carried the argument. Oddly enough, to judge from comments they made on various occasions, neither of the two principal architects of New Delhi, Sir Edward Lutyens and Sir Herbert Baker, saw much merit in the style they were obliged to work to!

We, however, were certainly not disappointed by what Lutyens and Baker had achieved. New Delhi is a genuine example of that rare phenomenon, the purpose-built capital city and, personally, I think it right to describe it as 'pretty successful'.

Remembering that motor vehicle usage was still in its infancy at the time the plans for New Delhi were being drawn, the arrangement of its avenues and thoroughfares was both bold and far-sighted. All its roads are characterised by immense width, by double rows of bordering trees and by carefully created vistas connecting the various points of interest so that no avenue merely disappears into the distance.

The central focus of the grand plan for New Delhi was the Viceroy's Palace, an edifice larger than any royal residence in Britain and in fact larger even than Louis XIV's vast palace of Versailles. The overall design of the Imperial City incorporated an approach to all the major government buildings along a grand avenue one and a half miles long called the 'Raj Path'. The Raj Path ends at the India Gate where there are several war memorials, the largest being in honour of the 70,000 Indian soldiers who died in the First World War.

Although it was unfortunate that shortage of time forced us to whip round New Delhi's magnificent imperial heritage at a breakneck pace, we were very lucky with our weather and were privileged to see all its wonders against an everchanging skyscape of stunning patterns and colours. Beginning with a rather unexceptional grey glow, the sky slowly ripened into a pearly pink luminescence before strangely and indiscernibly yellowing. Big puffy clouds, resembling those you'd see in a child's picture book, next built up, each outlined by some aerial artist with grey and gold borders as they became backlit by the dying sun. Meanwhile the yellows were turning orange as the cloud- whites dissolved into greys. Then, as a grand finale, the entire sky became blood red as the city began to turn on its lights.

Postscript

During our flight back home, I asked one of the cabin crew if it would be possible for the boys, in small groups of two or three at a time, to visit the cockpit at some convenient period of the flight so that the instruments and controls of the great airliner could be briefly explained. My request was cheerfully taken forward, the captain returning with the stewardess moments later to tell me in person that he would be delighted to oblige and would call us up once breakfast had finished. I was the last of the party to go up and was invited to sit in the co-pilot's seat and, whilst so enthroned, encouraged to use my cine camera to record the occasion.

That, of course, was in the Orwellian year of 1984 but I don't somehow think such a privilege would be as readily granted today. Indeed, I strongly suspect that in all likelihood I would have been turned down flat with frigid politeness and barely concealed pity at my naivety, with the negative response being blamed on some glibly quoted safety regulation.

Of course, over the years times change and new circumstances may make fresh rules inevitable but the matter does illustrate, I suggest, that advancing years bring with them retrogression as well as progress.